SPIRITUAL MESSAGES FROM

YAIDRON

SAVE THE WORLD FROM DESTRUCTION

HS PRESS

SPIRITUAL MESSAGES FROM
YAIDRON

SAVE THE WORLD FROM DESTRUCTION

RYUHO OKAWA

HS Press

Original title: *Yaidron no Reigen - Sekai no Houkai wo Kuitomeruniwa*
HS Press is an imprint of IRH Press Co., Ltd.
Tokyo
ISBN 13: 978-1-943928-23-1
ISBN 10: 1-943928-23-1

Contents

CHAPTER TWO

Tense Situation of Taiwan and Future Prospect of Coronavirus: UFO Reading 65 (Yaidron)

Preface

Here in Japan, there is the term "island-nation mentality." And these days, I have been feeling it as real as ever. No matter what happens in the world, people in Japan can do nothing but swim round and round in a confined space, like a tiny fish in a glass of water.

When it's time for an election, parties compete over dole-out policies. As for the media, they use the same old pattern to stir up people's fear. Can this shallow, frivolous country really do anything?

This book is a harsh scolding from the space being named Yaidron. To preserve the justice of this nation and the world, I must talk to the space beings and make the final decision. I will save those who believe in us and even those who do not if they accord with justice.

I believe 99.9 percent of the world's people will live the rest of their lives without knowing where this power of saving comes from.

Ryuho Okawa
Master & CEO of Happy Science Group
October 19, 2021

CHAPTER ONE

Spiritual Messages from Yaidron: Save the World from Destruction

Originally recorded in Japanese on August 24, 2021 at the Special Lecture Hall of Happy Science in Japan and later translated into English.

These spiritual messages were channeled through Ryuho Okawa. However, please note that because of his high level of enlightenment, his way of receiving spiritual messages is fundamentally different from other psychic mediums who undergo trances and are completely taken over by the spirits they are channeling. When Master Okawa channels spirits who do not speak Japanese, they are sometimes able to use vocabulary from his language center to communicate their spiritual messages in Japanese.

It should be noted that these spiritual messages are opinions of the individual spirits and may contradict the ideas or teachings of Happy Science Group.

Yaidron

Yaidron is a space being from Planet Elder in the Magellanic Clouds. His power is akin to the high-dimensional spirits of Earth's spirit world and he is akin to the *god of justice*. His role on Planet Elder is similar to a judge and politician of the highest grade, and he governs the justice and judgment there. He received teachings from El Cantare on a messiah-training planet, and is now a protector of Ryuho Okawa, who is El Cantare on earth. Yaidron is a being beyond his physical and spirit bodies, having an unlimited life span, and has also been attending to the rise and fall of Earth's civilizations, wars, and natural disasters.

In this chapter, there are a total of five interviewers from Happy Science, symbolized as A, B, C, D, and E in the order that they first appear.

1

Asking the Space Being Yaidron about the Future World Situation

RYUHO OKAWA

I would like to receive a spiritual message from Yaidron. We actually talked a little last night, but since it was getting late he said it would be better to do this today. So, we are now holding this session. These days, I feel the spiritual interview does not go well in a formal setting because the questions become the same as a common interview on earth. It somehow doesn't go well and the mood isn't right either. It's better if we do this while looking up at the night sky, but (in this indoor setting,) there is no mood. It's a little sad, but I hope that it will start rolling soon.

Yaidron's UFO that appeared in the sky on August 23, 2021.

I guess he quit our conversation last night to get some sleep for this morning [*laughs*]. I don't know exactly. I wonder if he works from the morning.

The world situation is changing and is becoming more fluid. So, we'd like to ask Mr. Yaidron if he sees anything we earthlings cannot even think of. Usually, we can only think about the immediate future, but we would be grateful if he could give us a more extended forecast.

Now, space being Mr. Yaidron, who is probably the most well-known at Happy Science, would you please join us for this recording?

[*About five seconds of silence.*]

2

Disorders in Afghanistan and Myanmar, and China's Ambition

The relation between the start of President Biden and the moves in Afghanistan and Myanmar

YAIDRON

Hmm. Hmm... Yes.

A

Good morning.

YAIDRON

Yes.

A

Thank you very much for this opportunity today.

Mr. Yaidron, I believe you are looking at the entire Earth from space. The latest hot topic in the world is the movement in Afghanistan. As soon as the U.S. troops withdrew, the Taliban took control of the country, and soon after that China and Russia got involved. I think the issue has entered a new phase now. So first, I would like to ask you the impact this issue will have on Earth.

YAIDRON

I think Happy Science was intending to solve the China problem and the Islam problem one by one, but the U.S. presidential election results made it impossible for you to do so, and you now have to handle both issues at the same time, right? Well, it turned out exactly how we had seen through. You have to face the situation where the China and Islam issues are entangled.

Last year, we had predicted various potential outcomes from the best to the worst about the presidential election, but it seems that the world is now moving toward fulfilling the worst-case scenario. I don't want you to see it as a coincidence.

The instant fall of Afghanistan by the hands of the Taliban is closely related to Biden becoming the president. The Taliban saw that Biden is a conciliatory man. So, in reality, the world will be more and more divided. Although Biden is trying to make the world harmonious and peaceful in his surface consciousness, what he is doing works to gradually divide the world even more. Well, this is something people with an IQ over 130 can understand, but those who are not on that level can't.

A

Triggered by the Afghan incident, I suppose further movements may occur in China, Russia, and Iran. I would like to ask you how we should read the changes in the few years to come.

YAIDRON

Before Afghanistan, there was a military coup in Myanmar around February this year. It was almost at the same time as the inauguration of the new U.S. president. Then, as soon as the U.S. started to withdraw troops from Afghanistan, the Taliban uprose all at once to take over Afghanistan. You need to assume that someone has been expecting all this and pulling the strings behind the scenes. So, your opponent is far more cunning than you imagine. All these incidents are linked and this is no coincidence. This didn't happen by chance. It's all connected. It was planned way before the presidential election had even started.

What's more, many movements have been occurring in various places to invite the withdrawal of the U.S. amid the worldwide spreading of the coronavirus. If there is someone planning all this from the macro perspective, then there is no way the Japanese government can handle this problem, seeing how deteriorated the brains of the government's central politicians have become.

A

Right.

YAIDRON

It's beyond their abilities.

A

Is it correct to assume that it's "a human brain on earth" that is planning it?

YAIDRON

No, it's beyond that.

A

"Beyond that."

YAIDRON

Brains beyond human's are involved.

A

I see.

B

What kind of people are involved in it on earth?

YAIDRON

Well, the rule of law in China is just a matter of implementing the "laws" that the leaders have come up with to benefit themselves. Xi Jinping aims to become the "emperor for life" and Putin of Russia also has such desires. So, someone is working to connect their desires. Master Okawa of Happy Science has been warning against the China-Russia alliance for several years, but no one in Japan had such a strategic perspective. Unfortunately, American journalists were also terribly foolish that they lost to the populists. So, it's quite disappointing.

The scary thing about Mr. Trump is that he's unpredictable. That is the scary part, and Xi Jinping was afraid of it, too. Even AI cannot determine what Trump would do. I'm not sure if this is the same as Shogi (Japanese chess) or Go (a checker-like game), but Mr. Trump makes extraordinary decisions and is unpredictable. In contrast, Mr. Biden is fairly predictable; if his abilities are input in AI, his actions will be predicted. Being predictable means traps can be set. The Taliban attack was too easy; Afghanistan fell in just about 10 days. It was also a little surprising how the American intelligence had such poor foreseeing abilities.

Future prospect of the "One Belt, One Road" Initiative

B

Mr. Yaidron, how do you see the Middle East region in the future, especially Afghanistan?

YAIDRON

At least Pakistan, Afghanistan, and Iran are now linked. This is the central part of the "One Belt, One Road" Initiative Xi Jinping is claiming. Now the question is how far it will extend from Iran. Will it extend to Turkey, Syria,

Greece, Italy, and even further down to Africa? Then, going down south, next will be Southeast Asia. I mean, China definitely had its eyes locked on Myanmar and it all went well. I think support from China was already given to the Myanmar military by the time the presidential election was held. I'm sure that meetings were held to discuss about the later schedule as well. So, the plan with Myanmar had already started about a year ago.

As for the Taliban, too, they can act so boldly and aggressively because they have the military logistics from China. They also have another backup from Russia. Russia is willing to cooperate if it means to weaken the U.S. Both China and Russia are involved, and also, Israel is getting very weak now. So, there has been a shift in the world.

In fact, the Taliban uprising and seizing power in Afghanistan and Myanmar's military regime destroying democracy were intended to invite the next chain reaction. This is a battle over the effectiveness between the movement to spread democratic values around the world promoted by the U.S. and Europe, and the pursuit of efficiency by the communist-like one-party controlled rule of man.

In a nation with no opposition, it's easy to control its people, but they cannot do the same in a global society unless they have others sharing the same opinions.

This is actually a world war. I believe that the world war started a little over a year and a half ago and is now still continuing. It is not just a virus war. As for the next step, there has been a war to destroy democracy by the military regime. Like the Othello or Reversi board game, they are trying to turn over democratic governments to expand their territory on Earth.

The "next weapon" after coronavirus

YAIDRON

There has already been a signal that the "next weapon" after coronavirus is anthrax. This has been revealed as there were deaths from anthrax in China. You may know anthrax from the attack that occurred in Japan in 1993 in which the Aum Shinrikyo religion dispersed it from their facility in Tokyo. There was also an incident in the U.S. in 2001, where a terrorist sent anthrax-containing envelopes to TV stations, newspaper companies, and to some senators.

In the case of coronavirus, China's original plan wasn't meant to start in Wuhan but was to bring the virus out of the country and spread it mainly in the U.S. to claim that it originated there. But an accident happened "by chance" for some reason, which I cannot clearly say, and people died within China, in Wuhan, revealing that the source was there. And now, for some reason, anthrax leaked out within China and killed several people. We cannot speak of how it happened, but it was to clarify that the "next attack" will be by anthrax.

A

I see. How will that anthrax attack widely occur in the future?

YAIDRON

I think it cannot be done so soon because only the chemical corps of the military can handle it.

A

Ah.

YAIDRON

So, as long as coronavirus is still conquering the world, I think they will stick to that. But at the same time, I think the anthrax attack will also occur in limited areas, in shocking places or countries China finds difficult to handle.

A

In limited areas. I see.

3

The Earth Crisis Seen by the Spiritual Eye

The reason why Islam is closer to materialist totalitarian nations

A

Going back to the earlier topic, you said the "brains beyond human's" are involved behind the scenes. What kind of thinking do they have?

YAIDRON

Hmm.

A

Is it correct to assume that they are connected to Ahriman (of the dark side of the universe)?

YAIDRON

Well, yes, in terms of the ones on the surface.

A

Oh.

YAIDRON

So, there are a lot more hidden behind.

A

A lot more?

YAIDRON

They'll appear one after another. It is a chance for them.

A

I see.

YAIDRON

The whole of Europe has been weakening.

A

Indeed.

YAIDRON

The U.S. is also weak.

A

Yes. As for you, Mr. Yaidron, if you read these "Ahriman-connected brains," what kind of final plot do you think they have?

YAIDRON

Hmm... Right now, China is trying to make the world believe, "China is the most advanced country in the world. They have conquered the coronavirus. They have the economic and military powers to save the world. They possess the highest level of science and technology. So, the next supreme ruler is China." Their plot is that only the countries who believe this and have turned to the side with China will continue to develop and prosper, while the anti-China countries will perish. And they are planning to bring the Muslim world into the plot.

Unfortunately, the Muslim world is shameful. The Uyghurs suffer terrible treatment, but other Muslims don't help them because it's a different country. They are demonstrating the worst aspect of Islam. Pakistan, Afghanistan, and even Iran should state that it's unforgivable to treat Uyghur Muslims in such a way, but they don't. They just want to secure their countries, even if it means sacrificing their fellow believers. China sees such aspects of Islam as they act. Islam is now pretty much like materialist totalitarian nations. China targets that weakness right on the spot.

Buddhism and Christianity have symbols for prayer, right? Buddhism has statues of Buddha, while Christianity has the cross and statues of Jesus and Mary. So, they both have the object of faith. But there is no object of worship in Islam; their mosques just have a dome with a hole in the ceiling through which the sky can be seen.

"Allah" is a general term for God, and no one has ever met Him. There are just two records about Allah. One is the Koran, in which Muhammad talks about the messages from God called Allah. The other is Hadith. Whether it's true or not, it describes that when Muhammad visited heaven, he met Jesus Christ in the second heaven and Abraham in the seventh, and above that was Allah. But no one has ever actually met Allah, and He has never come down. That is the reality of Islam. Islamic world achieved a scientific development in the Middle Ages, but now, how can I say...

Christianity and Buddhism have their own priests or ordained religious leaders, but Islam doesn't. Muslims are all lay believers. The current supreme leader, the president, and his subordinate officials may talk like clerics, but they are actually lay believers. Because there is no official priest and they are all lay believers, they are allowed to do all things the ordinary citizens are allowed to do.

China cunningly takes advantage of this weakness and is trying to turn the Muslim world into a communist one-party dictatorship or materialistic nations based on equality. They believe it doesn't matter if Mao Zedong or Xi Jinping sits in Allah's place. So, spotting that ideological similarity, they are trying to approach the Muslim world and be connected to them.

If the Taliban truly believe that God exists, they can't kill people or rape women, for example, because the Muslim teachings forbid killing and adultery. The mass rape of female Uyghur prisoners is not allowed according to Muslim teachings. But in reality, they ignore such teachings. This means they are just aiming to seize power in this world and to secure food.

The countries that have turned over to China are supported by Chinese arms, ammunition, and food. If it were not for China's aid, even Myanmar would not have succeeded in establishing a military regime. They made a coup because they knew they had a good chance of surviving even if the West imposed sanctions on them.

Once China has seized Myanmar, they can target India next. If China advances its troops to Myanmar, Pakistan, Nepal, Bhutan, and Tibet, then it'll be able to contain India. They've already reached out to Sri Lanka and established a Chinese military port there. I guess they are even thinking of war against India from all sides. So, China is thinking very seriously and professionally from the military point of view.

The danger of the "explosion" of the Earth Consciousness

A

Given that the "brains of the universe" are thinking of filling the Earth with a communist one-party dictatorship, what will happen after they have achieved it?

YAIDRON

Well, that's... That's hard to say because it's kind of a secret. We don't think everything will go as smoothly as they want. But we need to leave this situation until humans themselves determine what is good and evil in terms of the direction they should advance. So, I think many things will continue to happen until humans come to realize, "This is wrong."

A

Until we realize?

YAIDRON

Yes.

A

Listening to what you just said, I thought "freedom, democracy, and faith" that Master Okawa teaches at Happy Science will stand against it as the breakwater. Do you expect humans to recognize the importance of these concepts in the end?

YAIDRON

China advocates "dictatorship, equality through poverty, and atheism and materialism," right? They believe these concepts are more effective, and there is nothing wrong with advocating these if this world is all there is. In a nutshell, they think, "People are just tools. Those in power can use their people when they are useful, tax them when it's possible, and let them die when they want to save food."

The Nazis have become a thing of the past, and people no longer understand the concept or read historical books about them. In China, there is no report, literature, or film work on them. China only has one color, which is Chinese patriotism.

A

I see.

YAIDRON

This is going to be the next storm. To make things worse, you need to know that climate change is also involved. There was heavy rain in Germany, China, and also Japan. And now, there is flooding in Tennessee, U.S., and more than 20 people have died. In the U.S., it's unusual that people are killed by the flooding of a river, although it's common for an area to be flooded by a hurricane.

Some unusual events are going on, and I think there is a movement to accelerate things. In terms of such bizarre events, you may have to watch closely over the movement of China's satellites.

A

Do you mean China's satellites and climate change are connected in some ways?

YAIDRON

That's possible. By now, it is possible to make it rain artificially. So, right now, I think China is "practicing" and trying to control climate change.

A

Talking about the Earth Consciousness that you once mentioned, if humans continue to try controlling even climate change, what will the Earth Consciousness do?

YAIDRON

It will "explode."

A

Explode?

YAIDRON

It's going to "explode" soon. Before long, Yahweh-like God of Wrath—not like the gentle Yaidron—should appear.

A

The God of Wrath.

YAIDRON

At some point. Well, we are the ones to set fire, anyway. It's going to happen very soon.

A

Soon?

YAIDRON

Yes. At your convenience.

A

Will that be related to the natural environment?

YAIDRON

That is not yet decided. Right now, China is practicing how to accurately start a wildfire at a specific location or accurately cause a flood. But they still don't have good precision. They use viruses, right? They also use anthrax, wildfire, and flooding. They're doing all kinds of things.

A

I see.

C

Is it likely that the wildfires in the U.S. and the floods in other countries are caused by such Chinese weapons?

YAIDRON

It may not be called a weapon, but if they plan it, they can do it. There are many Chinese people already living in the U.S., and a lot of them are spies of the People's Liberation Army. They can of course use weapons, but if they want to spare money, they can do it with just a single matchstick [*laughs*].

The effect of the emergence of a new island in the Ogasawara Islands

B

Now that you have talked about climate change and abnormal weather, I would like to ask you a question related to them. Recently, there has been news of a new volcanic island discovered in the Ogasawara Islands of Japan. I wonder if there is any possibility of a continental shift happening in the future. Is there anything you can tell us about it?

YAIDRON

Well, it may take a little longer before it happens. You know that the final judgment of the Earth Consciousness includes the sinking and surfacing of continents. But in reality, people who are alive now cannot even think about it. So, let me just tell you that if one place rises, another place sinks.

B

Some sources say that the area where an island is now surfacing is the western edge of where the Mu continent used to be. It may be that the former continent of Mu is about to appear again. But as you have just said, does the emergence of a new continent mean that an existing continent will sink?

YAIDRON

I think volcanic eruptions will happen before that. A number of volcanos will probably erupt. I guess that will be first.

C

For example, Mt. Fuji?

YAIDRON

Well, we have to think about whether that's a good thing or a bad thing for you. Rather than Mt. Fuji, you would instead hope Mt. Paektu (in North Korea) to erupt first, wouldn't you?

4

"World War III" and the Future of Taiwan and Japan

Are we in World War III?

D

You mentioned that Afghanistan, Myanmar, and other countries are all connected to each other. Is it correct to assume that, from your bird's-eye view from the universe, you have a feeling of the Third World War coming?

YAIDRON

No, I'm not saying I foresee it or feel it. I am saying it has already started.

D

Yes.

YAIDRON

The war has already begun in a different style. It is no longer the same as previous wars.

D

I see. In that situation, how do you see the postwar regime of Japan? For example, the Japan Self-Defense Forces have not yet been mobilized to evacuate embassy personnel from Afghanistan.

YAIDRON

Well, they are just sending transport planes.

D

Yes, with the help of British military aircraft.

YAIDRON

They are sending transport planes to rescue the Japanese residents and to allow the evacuation of the Afghans working at the Japanese embassy. It is a little unusual that Japan steps into things this far. I hope they wouldn't be shot down by a bazooka or something. It would be shameful for the Japan Self-Defense Forces if their planes were shot down by the Taliban's shoulder-held weapon. It would really be a shame, so I hope they will be careful.

I guess they don't have escorts. Normally when a transport plane goes, some jet fighters should be escorting the plane. But they are sending the aircraft with no escort, on the assumption that it's a peaceful time. In reality, you never know what you will get when flying over certain countries, even when these countries are not yet in a state of war. Unless you keep the air route secret, you never know what is awaiting. What's more, the airport is also targeted.

D

Right. Compared to other countries, Japan is far behind in terms of evacuation operations. I think Japan is the only country that is truly slow and can't cope with world situations.

YAIDRON

On top of that, it's possible that the Japanese Communist Party may come into administration in the next political situation. Such a time is nearing, so it is very dangerous. The world map will change considerably if the Japanese Communist Party gains even one ministerial post.

A message to Japan, a country that doesn't take any action

C

Looking at how Japan doesn't take any action, sometimes Master Okawa bemoans, saying that Japan is really hopeless. The majority of Japanese people are indifferent to the suffering of the world's people, and it just can't be helped. Do you have any messages to such a country?

YAIDRON

People of Japan think their current political regime was created and forced by the occupation forces after World War II, and they don't think it reflects a value that they have traditionally upheld. So, they have been indifferent to the current situation. It is as if they are saying, "You are the one to have forced us into this political regime, so it's your duty to defend Japan."

Coincidentally, this time, the Taliban took over the capital of Afghanistan and even seized control of the Afghan media. At that time, U.S. President Biden said, as part of his excuse, "This did unfold more quickly than we had anticipated." But he also mentioned that the U.S.

arms supply would make no difference if Afghan troops would not stand up to protect their own country. He said, "American troops cannot and should not be fighting in a war and dying in a war that Afghan forces are not willing to fight for themselves." This coincides with what he (the guardian spirit) said in his spiritual messages. In them, he said he could not see why the U.S. should protect Japan if Japan itself is not willing to protect its own country. This means should a war happens next, the battlefield will be Japan, and whoever takes over Japan will consequently be the victor—China or the U.S.

On top of this, Russia is showing its moves to add a piece to it by trying to turn the four northern islands into military bases. If China and Russia team up to take over Japan under the pretext of preparing for an invasion by the U.S., it means they feel dissatisfied with how World

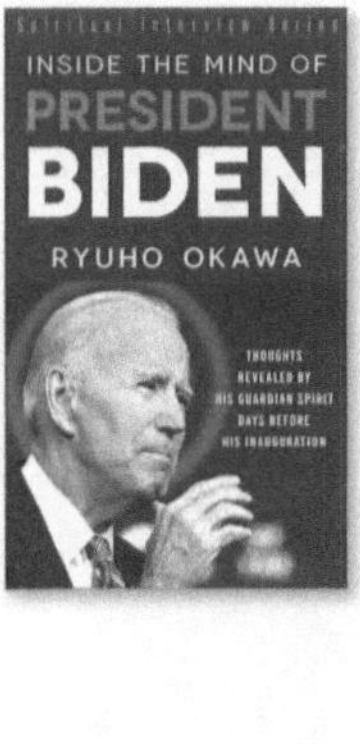

Inside the Mind of President Biden
(Tokyo: HS Press, 2021)

War II had ended and want to redraw the world map anew. They think it is unacceptable how the U.S. took Japan all by themselves.

The First Island Chain stretches in the waters near Japan. But if, as China envisions, the Second Island Chain is shifted as far as to Hawaii with the U.S. military line retreating to Hawaii, then Japan will not be able to survive unless they manage to withstand the invasion and colonialism of either China or Russia, or both.

What China is aiming to do by taking advantage of Biden's weakness

D

You talked about Biden's response to Afghanistan. Some say that there were mistakes in assessing information on the U.S. side. But as you just said, or as it was revealed in the spiritual messages, maybe he went ahead with the withdrawal plan knowing what would happen. Even if it may leave Afghanistan in chaos, Biden may have been determined to withdraw the American troops regardless because the U.S. can no longer commit itself. So perhaps, similar things may happen in East Asia.

YAIDRON

That's right. Or rather, it is their aim. That's what China is aiming for. Taiwan is becoming more and more anxious, right?

D

Yes. Taiwan is also being threatened.

YAIDRON

The opposition party is gaining momentum, and this is a chance to get rid of Tsai Ing-wen, right? It implies, "If you seek protection from the U.S., you will end up like Afghanistan."

D

The Chinese government even boldly tells that Taiwan needs to learn lessons from the Afghan case.

YAIDRON

In a way, they are saying that to Japan as well. Next, the Chinese spokesman will probably announce that Japan is not safe as long as Japan has U.S. military bases. They might state things like, "Countries with U.S. military bases are not safe, while countries without U.S. military bases are safe."

D

Looking at this situation, I assume that Biden will take a similar approach to the Senkaku Islands. If the Japanese forces don't act, then there is a high chance of him not mobilizing the American troops, although they have agreed that Article 5 of the Japan-U.S. Security Treaty applies to the Senkaku Islands. I believe the Japanese government must assume that this is his true thought.

YAIDRON

I guess Japan's stance would be to just follow the American troops. Once the American troops are mobilized to surround the Senkaku Islands, they will send the Japan Self-Defense Forces to follow them, escort, and give them supplies and just tag along with the American troops. But unfortunately, the U.S. is no longer the country it used to be.

I think the reason why Mr. Trump had decided to withdraw the U.S. troops from Afghanistan is open to discussion. Of course, one reason was to cut military expenses. He thought the U.S. needed to revitalize its economy by reducing its budget deficit and become a strong country economically, to maintain its military power. For him, the U.S. withdrawal would go hand in hand with America's economic reform, including the revival of the domestic industry. But Mr. Biden cannot connect these issues, and he separates the military from the economy.

When Mr. Xi Jinping visited the U.S., he was invited to Trump's resort in Florida for dinner. When the main dish finished and the dessert was served, a memo was delivered, saying that the U.S. military had just fired missiles at Syria. It was when Xi Jinping was about to eat his dessert. That was a threat, a 100 percent threat. Mr. Trump was a scary person who could do such a thing. So, even if Trump said that he would withdraw troops, you never knew what he would actually do. In contrast, it doesn't seem like Biden can do such a thing, and this weakness is completely taken advantage of. Chinese also play the board game Go, so they read the opponent's next moves.

How the Japanese companies benefited China by dividing politics and economy

A

I would like to ask you further in connection to military power. Recently, there's been a shortage of semiconductors, and it is said that cars and electrical products cannot be manufactured. A little earlier, in Japan, there was a sudden fire at a semiconductor factory. In short, if cars don't work, it means weapons don't work either. Is there any strategy of China behind this situation?

YAIDRON

If the main factories are in China, it's obvious that everything will be confiscated. With the U.S. imposing sanctions on China, if Japan takes part in the joint military operations with the U.S. based on the Japan-U.S. alliance, then the factories of the Japanese car manufacturers will all be confiscated and become Chinese. So, of course, you will no longer be able to use those factories.

Also, when the Japanese companies were all trying to relocate their factories to Southeast Asia, the coronavirus suddenly spread there, and the military coup occurred, creating political instability. In this way, China has created a situation where the Japanese would want to escape from Southeast Asia.

But up to this point, things have been proceeding as we had expected.

A

In that case, it seems like the Japanese companies are unknowingly helping the reinforcement of Chinese military power.

YAIDRON

I don't think they are doing so "unknowingly."

A

They are knowingly contributing?

YAIDRON

They have been aware of it, but they kept insisting, "Politics is politics, economy is economy." That is how Japan has been since the end of World War II. Japan used to be described as a country of a "first-rate economy with third-rate politics" until the end of the bubble economy. It relied on the U.S. to protect Japan and instead concentrated on boosting its economy.

A

Many politicians in the current Liberal Democratic Party of Japan think that the Japanese economy is closely connected to China. I think we need politicians who have more wisdom to consider the economy from the perspective of national defense. I wonder if it's really all right for the current administration to continue.

YAIDRON

Well [*smiles wryly*], whatever administration may continue, it's probably not all right. To say the least, it's a pretty shameful situation that Japan is unable to do anything, despite knowing that a Chinese hacking group has been hacking into more than 200 companies of Japan, especially military, electronics and computer-related companies; it has been stealing information for years.

The possibility of a nuclear missile embarking on the Chinese satellite

A

I think China has already surpassed Japanese military power by now. As for Japan, to seriously work to improve its defense, what kind of industries or technology should we develop in the next few years or 10 years to come? I'd like to know if you have any new perspectives.

YAIDRON

If I were a Chinese spokesman, as soon as Japan shows any signs of turning against China, I would simply say, "We can even fire a nuclear missile from satellites." Then Japan wouldn't be able to do anything because Japan doesn't have the ability to shoot down a satellite.

B

I think you just mentioned a crucial point. Do you mean that Chinese satellites are armed with nuclear weapons?

YAIDRON

The possibility is...

B

So, it's possible.

YAIDRON

The possibility is high. They already have such capability. I can't talk about it in detail now because it's related to the decision of whether or not we will ultimately take action.

When there is a normal military coup, they claim that other nations should not intervene in the foreign countries' domestic issues. At the same time, they bring out the issue of ethnic autonomy and claim that just as China allows ethnic autonomy, Myanmar and Afghanistan should also govern themselves on their own and should not allow foreign intrusion. They are trying to expand their campaign to kick out foreign countries in this way.

Even if you ask us what we can do under such circumstances, where the military is cracking down upon its citizens and protestors using tanks and machine guns, well...

Actually, I was told off by Master Okawa just yesterday. I made my appearance last night, and Aide to Master & CEO Shio said to Master Okawa, "It might be a good idea to talk with the space people, who might be here." But Master replied, "No need. They don't work anyway. They aren't willing to do anything." Well, it is partially true. If the space beings were to intervene in the situation where a country's military is abusing its citizens and start to annihilate the army, it could only be seen as a "space war." It is difficult to intervene unless there is more of a justifying reason, especially when the existence of space beings itself still hasn't been clearly accepted.

We don't mind being exposed of intervening if a nuclear war starts, or of shooting down ICBMs if they are launched. In reality, we have shot down a missile before, but people just thought it was an accident. We actually did it. So, if the situation is that serious, we'll intervene immediately. But if it's just the level in which the government is unable to control their own military... I wonder how earthlings think of the fact that they are at such a low level as a country.

What is needed to change the Japanese "it's not my business" mentality

B

According to what you just said, I understand that a certain level is needed to intervene this Earth, for the space beings who are protecting the God of the Earth—such as you, Mr. Yaidron, Mr. Metatron, and Mr. R. A. Goal. Even when China is now spreading the coronavirus around the world, or even if they do use biological weapons like anthrax that you mentioned earlier, or chemical weapons, is it still not at the level for space beings to intervene?

YAIDRON

The origin of the coronavirus is still not acknowledged, right? Everyone is just insisting on their own theory, saying that it started in the U.S. or started somewhere else or claiming that it is of a natural cause. China is bold enough to say that it came from abroad via frozen food [*laughs*]. In the past, there was indeed an incident in Japan where some frozen food from China contained some chemicals.

In a way, you may feel envious that a country can say all sorts of excuses for any criticisms that arise. You see, Chinese people can lie. They actively do so. North and South Koreans can also lie, and so can people in all Islamic regions in the desert, which is now a hot topic. On the other hand, Japanese people can't lie openly. They can separate private-self and public-self when they act, so that they can lie indirectly. This is Japan's attitude. This is often referred to as a characteristic of those in the Rear Heaven of the Spirit World. Although they cannot lie straightforwardly, they lie indirectly by separating their private-self and public-self.

To give you an example, Japan has been endlessly discussing about how the Japan Self-Defense Forces are not military, although it's obvious that they are. By insisting that they are not military forces, the national defense of Japan is impeded for sure.

Also, when the U.S. president released what seemed to be UFO footage, the then Japanese defense minister ordered the Air Self-Defense Force by saying something along the lines of, "Now that the American president, or the Pentagon, released such information, collect as much evidence as possible, just in case you have encountered such objects, although I myself don't believe in UFOs." He said like this as though it had nothing to do with him personally; everything is other people's business. But for the U.S., it is a matter of preparing for a case of an invasion from outer space, as well as from foreign nations using some technology while pretending to be aliens.

Japanese people need to change this "it's not my business" mentality. Your political party (Happiness Realization Party) is the only one that acts on real intentions.

Well, you have been actively speaking out about the coronavirus as well as China's territorial ambition. Some mass media have started to follow your opinions about these issues, but they always leave room for escape.

When a nation doesn't defend itself, despite having the power to do so, then it's questionable whether we should go as far as to intervene. It is the same as the police can't do anything for the people who commit suicide or jump off a cliff. I mean, people can die if they want to. It is your own choice to go to a cliff up north and dive into the Sea of Japan. Everyone is not watched over all the time. You can't stop a samurai from killing himself by *seppuku* (honorable death) if that's his wish.

So, you need to change your mindset. I suppose that's why Ame-no-Mioya-Gami (Japanese Father God) has come down to Happy Science recently and is speaking about the spirit of *bushido*. I think He means that Japan should essentially tell good from evil and act resolutely, and that the postwar regime is not necessarily right. But even if Master Okawa says that, I don't think Japan will make a move. So, I think a bit more tragic situation would occur in Japan.

A

Do you mean that such a situation will arise in the next few years?

YAIDRON

As soon as Japan does something to try to look good, they will be met by a huge reaction. So, it's more likely that they end up shutting up or running back into a hole like a prairie dog.

If Taiwan falls, next is Okinawa, then the mainland of Japan

A

What kind of tragic situations do you mean? Is it a natural phenomenon or a military matter?

YAIDRON

China can attack Taiwan today if they want to. The distance between them is short and the south coast of China is full of missiles. If China launches the missiles, a war can start even today. Naturally, Taiwan will fight back. They will of course fight back, but they can only hold it for a week or 10 days. Taiwan will perish unless the UN passes a resolution and the U.S. and European countries come to help.

Will Japan be able to decide to join them in defending Taiwan during this critical time of a week or 10 days? If Japan decides to participate in the defense, what level of defense will they take? Would they provide logistical support of oil to the U.S. and European troops or bring back casualties to hospitals in Japan? Or will Japan only provide food aid? Nothing has been decided yet.

A

If Japan abandons Taiwan, the next step of China will be...

YAIDRON

They will seize Okinawa. Once Taiwan is seized, Okinawa will be taken next. This is definite.

But in the meantime, China is planning a withdrawal strategy of the U.S. army from Japan, just as they did for Afghanistan. They are increasing the number of communists and leftists in Okinawa and are promoting the campaign against U.S. military bases. At the moment, there are protests against the relocation of U.S. base from Futenma to Henoko, so they are taking this opportunity to instigate them by saying, "We could be involved in a war," and are demanding for the removal of the base and the prohibition of nuclear missiles.

They even protested against the deployment of Osprey helicopters. Ospreys have the power to fly to the Senkaku Islands and even come back with the people from the islands. A helicopter with a short cruising distance will crash halfway. Cruising distance is a vital issue in the Air Self-Defense Force. But whether they're aware of this or not, the local residents just protest. They only worry, saying "What if Osprey crashes?" Well, even a UFO will crash when it falls, so it can't be helped.

A

There is not much talk about what would come after Okinawa. What will happen if Okinawa falls?

YAIDRON

Well, they probably intend to take entire Japan.

A

"Entire Japan."

YAIDRON

Yes, but Russia will move too if China tries to take Japan.

A

They will move at the same time?

YAIDRON

That's why Russia has been trying to fortify the Northern Territories. They will take Hokkaido first.

The Japan's Self-Defense Forces won't be able to deal with both the south and the north simultaneously. During the Cold War era, they defended Hokkaido and the Sea of Japan side of Tohoku, but now they have been shifted greatly toward the south.

You created the Happiness Realization Party in 2009 to save Japan from such threats, but sadly the Japanese people did not take it seriously at all. So, Japan has set the schedule for its destruction.

5
What Is Needed for Japan to Be Awakened

"There is no need to protect the nations where evil is rampant"

A

At the beginning of this session, you said that you don't intend to allow China to complete its ambition to dominate the world by dictatorship.

YAIDRON

We intend to protect good nations that are based on faith.

A

So, the condition is that people have faith.

YAIDRON

Yes. And also, the nations where people are trying to establish justice on earth. There is no need to protect the nations where evil is rampant.

In Japan, Prime Minister Suga (at the time of the recording) visited Hiroshima and Nagasaki on the days of the atomic bombing, but soon after that, both cities had heavy rains due to a linear rainband. I don't think the rains were necessarily due to a Chinese weapon but a manifestation of the will of the Japanese gods. They are demanding self-reflection from Japan because a "No More Hiroshima" movement can open the way for Japan to be occupied again. Likewise, natural disasters frequently hit Fukushima, where a nuclear power plant accident happened. I think the Japanese Shinto gods and those who are close to them are demanding self-reflection from Japan.

A

When you say "faith," I think you are not speaking of a superficial one but a real faith—belief in Lord El Cantare, the Creator. But most people in Japan don't have faith in the first place, and even the U.S. is now becoming closer to a materialistic nation. Will such nations be saved as they are now?

YAIDRON

Another point is that people are being deceived. Ever since the time of Deng Xiaoping, China has been pretending to be developing greatly in a planned way under the modified socialism, giving the impression that the communist bloc is doing better. People had a similar impression when the Soviet Union was growing. There still are many people who think that way.

The mass media in the U.S. only reveal negative incidents, and they often write about how bad the American economy is, but China hides their own bad news. They even underreport the number of deaths.

In North Korea, for instance, no one has contracted the coronavirus, right? Although their official number of infected cases is zero, some top officials got fired for failures in coronavirus prevention. They were replaced. Similarly, in China, the number of infected cases hasn't increased at all from 100,000. Such lies can be left alone, and world justice is not properly applied in those countries because there is no media democracy. Free speech was expected to spread with the Internet society, but this also is controlled.

The Taliban in Afghanistan is the same. They are killing reporters and journalists one after another because their pictures and news reports can be posted on the Internet. They try to get rid of anyone that might report on them. The same is true in Myanmar. So, exposing evil through media, such as papers and images, won't work to bring down the rulers because they think nothing of killing others. Such means only work in democratic countries.

So, the world is really going in the wrong direction. Although Happy Science has been publishing many books and producing movies, the percentage of people who read and watch them is unfortunately low. In the case of TV, the rating of a news program is at least 10 percent, so 10 million people watch it (across Japan). Sometimes, tens of millions of people watch it. With such numbers, you can leave an impact on society. But public opinions are not influenced by the books and movies of Happy Science as they are now.

Of course, we are considering when we should intervene, but after all, we could end up just offering a prophecy, and that's it.

The reason for doing the primitive battle against Ahriman's attack

C

At the beginning of this session, you mentioned that some beings who have intelligence beyond humans on earth—most probably those related to Ahriman—are obviously active behind the scenes. What do such existences of the dark side of the universe ultimately intend to do by changing the values of the entire Earth? It appears as if they are leading a rebellion against El Cantare, but what are they really aiming to do?

YAIDRON

If you look at world history, it's obvious that the dark ages have come many times across the history of humanity. So, it's difficult to make such evil disappear completely.

To put it in a Chinese context, however, a "revolution" is certain to occur at such times. But until the rise of revolution, the dark age will continue. There are conditions for a revolution to take place. Current China is a "revolutionary regime," so conditions must be met for a counter-revolution to occur.

These conditions for a counter-revolution are not created enough in Japan. Looking at the character of the Japanese now, even if something bad really happens, such as not only the Senkaku Islands but also Okinawa being taken, they may not go into war.

A

I'd like to ask you further on how to fight against Ahriman. Recently, in addition to the space beings like you, a spirit named Doutei-ko nyan-nyan, or the goddess Lake Dongting, has appeared in Happy Science. Is there anything you can reveal to us on how you are going to connect space and the Spirit World to change the Earth?

YAIDRON

Hahaha [*laughs*]. In a way, we are sorry for doing such a primitive battle. I do think that unleashing floods and locusts are a little primitive way of fighting, but it would not leave us a good aftertaste if earthlings were to think that "monsters" came from outer space to rampage the world.

It is very difficult to guide earthlings to change their hearts. There are so many people who don't reflect on themselves. They don't practice self-reflection. They don't do it at all.

Japan is the same. Japan is definitely moving toward pushing religion to extinction. You need to be more aware that Japan is being incorporated into China as if being sucked in a vacuum cleaner.

China boldly says that the Senkaku Islands are the core interests of China, or Okinawa—or the Ryukyu Islands—are the core interests of China. Right? It's like people insisting, "The neighboring land is mine." Normally, that would give rise to a dispute. But China is a country that continues to say things like that with no hesitation.

Japan itself needs to be reformed, but the "gods of wrath" may be necessary to do so.

A

"Gods of wrath"?

YAIDRON

The ancient methods are too simplistic, and we don't think they are very beautiful. We don't really like the gods who praise the ones who obey and punish the ones who don't. That is just too simple. But I feel that people wouldn't understand unless we take such measures. This is actually the same level as training animals. It's like training dogs to "sit" and "shake hands" before feeding them. It is a little sad.

A

Is it all right to assume that you, Mr. Yaidron, are one of the "gods of wrath"?

YAIDRON

No, no. I am not.

A

You are not.

YAIDRON

I just do what I need to do to carry out my purpose. I myself, alone, have the power to destroy all nuclear weapons depots and the like.

A

All of them?

YAIDRON

Yes. I know all of their locations as well as the number of weapons. So, I can do it. But how I do it is another question.

How to battle against China, who aims for world domination

B

The People's Republic of China was established in 1949, and the year 2049 will be its 100th anniversary. China is aiming to dominate the world by then and is now expanding its hegemony by working together with Russia and receiving help from the dark side of the universe.

This may be a difficult question to answer, but looking into 2049 and 2050s from the present, what kind of situation do you think we are in now? I would also appreciate it if you could tell us about what kind of future you are envisioning toward 2050.

YAIDRON

If the current situation continues as it is, the global population on Earth might be reduced to half. If you add the Chinese, Muslims, and those who will come under Chinese rule, the total population will amount to about 4 billion. The total population of the U.S., Europe, and other democratic countries will be about 4 billion, too. So, it could be a battle between 4 billion versus 4 billion, in which one or the other will perish.

Frankly speaking, however, since El Cantare has descended on Earth, we are planning to let China collapse.

B

Until recently, information was controlled within the country, and any kind of bad news was not reported in China. But since last year, there have been more reports about the massive flooding, heavy rain, food crises, and so on. Do you have any idea of what is happening right now inside China?

YAIDRON

Inflation is happening, and food shortages are quite serious.

China is showing their support to reduce the amount of CO_2 emission, but they are doing so to strangle developed countries, and they themselves haven't done much to actually reduce it. They prioritize making a living because if industry stops, they can't sustain themselves. They are planning to delay their own action until 2060 while demanding developed countries to achieve their goals by 2050. All they have to do is for the Bureau of Statistics to continue making false announcements. I think that's their plan.

Well, it's too bad. If the revolution of Happy Science had been more successful, both religiously and politically, Japan would have been more different, and it would have had a bigger influence over the world. But unfortunately, Happy Science has yet to reach the point where it can influence global trends. It's too bad.

Also, while we shouldn't hope for this, time is near when the Japanese mass media will crash. Many newspaper companies will go under, and some TV stations are at risk too. This is another factor. There is also a question of whether the banking system can survive, not only domestically but also globally. The Myanmar issue actually involves money problems, as well as military power. People have problems because banks don't have enough money, and they can't withdraw or transfer money.

One way of fighting China is this: China is maneuvering to dominate the world like a frog competing against the ox.

But according to the art of war, a long-stretched military line can fall into confusion if its middle part is attacked. To achieve his ambition of world domination, Xi Jinping is extending the battle line further and further by giving financial aid and military support to various countries, so if we make something crash, then China should collapse entirely.

Even if they can make false statistics, the reality is different. There are probably about 400 million people who suffer from the food shortage out of the 1.4 billion people in China. When there are 400 million people who cannot afford to eat, how can they continue to support countries in Africa, Southeast Asia, and Muslim countries?

Another factor is the Chinese public officials' non-productive activities such as espionage. They are gathering information on individuals and monitoring all their activities. This doesn't produce any value at all. This was something that East Germany—a friendly country of the Soviet Union in the past—used to do. They were doing surveillance for many years to see if there were any spies or if any information was leaked to the West. Nothing was produced from this activity, so the economy got worse, and eventually, the country collapsed.

So, we are thinking of collapsing the Chinese economy as one of the most peaceful ways to solve the problem. China is greedy, so we will just let them get even greedier and cause the collapse of the Chinese economy when the battle line is fully extended. This is one way.

This year, there will probably be some personnel reshuffling in China for vice president and prime minister posts. Last year, Premier Li Keqiang said that 600 million people in China are living on a monthly income of about ¥17,000 or US$150. He revealed how China is not a rich country, so his dismissal is certain. He told the truth because as prime minister, he thought he had to let people know the truth. If people believe false reports only and think that everything is developing, they'll be in big trouble. So, there are 600 million people of families who are living on a monthly salary of US$150.

On top of that, massive flooding occurred and affected 30 million people, and a swarm of locusts ate up the crops. Can you imagine the impact of these events? The price of pork is rising and causing inflation, but they claim that it is a sign of economic development and add it to their calculations. They even count inflation as part of economic development. They are doing such things, so

I'm sure their economic collapse will happen at some point in the future. Therefore, an economic approach is one possible way of attacking them.

However, the U.S. has a domestic problem. They tried hard to oust Mr. Trump by trapping him in the alleged Russia scandal. In that way, they tried to draw people's attention away from Biden's money issue with China. Biden received funds from China via his family member. Because he is trying to hide that fact, it is highly likely that China's issue won't be exposed during the Biden administration. If he tried to reveal everything, he would be in trouble. This was the worst part of him, but even the American mass media were taken in.

To counter this, we can only pray that Jewish money will strike back. We just hope that Jewish money will strike back at Chinese money and regain control of the U.S. economy. Chinese money has largely entered the mass media, carrying out lobbying activities in the U.S.; China is working quite strategically. They are a tough opponent.

The difference in attitude between China and Japan toward a unified nation

A

What you are saying really makes sense. As a rule of history, a country that becomes too strong or too big will surely fall. For example, the Qin dynasty of Qin Shi Huang did not last long. In addition to the economy, are there any other weak points associated with the size or strengths of a country?

YAIDRON

China is a little different from how the Japanese think. In China, creating a unified dynasty is a dream one wants to achieve. Reigning and controlling a huge country with a large population is their dream; it's their ideal. If they fail to do so, the country will easily be divided into about six kingdoms, and wars will go on and on, and foreign countries will come to attack them. That's how they used to be in their history. Because they don't like such warring times, they want to be united as a strong nation, which is a good thing for them.

In the past, Japan, too, had a time when people strived to build a unified nation, but things would be tough when wars broke out. Nobunaga Oda was killed before he could unify the country. Even in a country like Japan, wars occur at such times. During the rule of Ieyasu Tokugawa, although the country was unified, its regime was very similar to today's China. Japan's economy did not develop at all for more than 260 years. Just imagine a future where the current zero GDP growth lasts for 300 years.

A

The Tokugawa Shogunate was actually extremely vulnerable to invasion by other countries.

YAIDRON

In a sense, Japan was protected by the sea. Japan knew the pattern of foreign invasion: Once they open their country to (trade with) foreign countries, missionaries will come, followed by the arrival of the army and occupation. Japan knew their way, so it was vigilant and allowed only the city of Nagasaki to be opened. The leaders of the Meiji Restoration took action because they feared Japan could be colonized by foreign countries. It's a shame that a nation where people worked hard in those times is now totally indifferent to world affairs and does not take any action.

The reason why souls that fell to hell do not perish

A

Let me change the subject. Ahriman is now intervening in the Earth using Xi Jinping, but is such intervention allowed? Shouldn't it be prohibited under the Space Treaty?

YAIDRON

Well, there are heaven and hell on other planets in the universe as well. If a law was to be created saying, "Souls that fell to hell shall perish," then there wouldn't be such thing as hell, so that is one way. However, our souls are given freedom, so we can choose good or evil. People will end up in hell if their amount of evil overweighs their good. It is like a prison, a detention center, and a hospital. And as these fallen souls reside in hell for too long, they start to make their own kind of rules and form various groups.

If El Cantare decided that fallen souls must perish, then the problem could be solved. But most people have the potential to come up to heaven if they repent. And when there is no chance for them to repent, the entire civilization will perish. Actually, there have been such events in the past. When Atlantis was taken over by devils in its final days, the continent of Atlantis itself sank. The same thing happened with the Mu continent. God let people with the right mind escape and had them create a new civilization elsewhere. God had done so in the past, and this is how He deals with the matter; God manages the world on earth and does not touch the Spirit World.

This is, in a sense, a guarantee that allows humans to have the same creative ability as God. If humans were like robots, inputted only to make specific decisions, then they wouldn't end up in hell. However, the truth is that we are given the freedom to choose from at least two or more values. This is how our wisdom is refined. So, it is not a complete collapse.

There is also the aspect of effectively using evil. When some kind of change is required, evil can arise along the way, so there are times when you must accept it for a certain period of time. Sometimes the good can be purified further by the presence of evil. Unless evil arises, it will be difficult to distinguish between good and evil. Because of that, there is a certain amount of allowance for evil to appear for a short period of time. In a way, by sending out various kinds of information, we are now trying to expose the evil thoughts of evil space beings and their servants on Earth.

Military forces are necessary to fight against evil and for a nation to be independent

YAIDRON

The Taliban have the Islamic faith, and they are fundamentalists. The word "Taliban" means the students of the school of God, so for them, it's like Happy Science University. But they are following fundamentalism. The starting point of fundamentalism lies in the fact that Muhammad destroyed all 360 gods (idols) in Mecca through an armed revolution and established a monotheistic religion; he established a state religion by winning a war. That is why they have a great affinity with Mao Zedong's military-first policy.

Although they know that killing people, in general, is wrong, they believe that fighting to get rid of foreign powers accords with justice. Along the way, they kill citizens as well. People in foreign countries feel very sorry for those who are desperately wishing to escape the country and are rushing to the airport and other places, but from the Taliban's eyes, those people are possessed by devils and are trying to live out without repenting to God. For the Taliban, such people must be dragged back to be punished or to be killed.

However, for those who are watching TV, a country that citizens wish to abandon, a country from which people want to flee, is a bad country. This is a simple indication. On the other hand, a country to which people want to flee or which people want to choose to seek asylum is a good country. This is a very simple litmus test. The Taliban don't understand that these people are escaping because their country is bad. This is the problem. That is why international sanctions and condemnation are necessary.

The guardian spirit of Aung San Suu Kyi called on the Japan Self-Defense Forces to come for help in her recent spiritual message (*Will There Be Peace in Myanmar?: Spiritual Interviews with the Guardian Spirits of Aung San*

Suu Kyi and Gen. Min Aung Hlaing and Messages from Shakyamuni Buddha), but Japan doesn't intend to intervene in Myanmar. They actually can't because there are many Japanese companies in Myanmar, and they don't know what kind of retaliation these companies would meet if they mobilized the Self-Defense Forces. This is Japan's position.

Military forces are not all evil, and they are actually necessary to fight against evil. If there were no police, the city would be dominated by Mafia, which shouldn't be allowed. Police should be stronger than the gangs. Even if the military made mistakes in the past, it still is necessary for a country to be independent.

If people do not approve of the military and only accept the Self-Defense Forces on the condition that they

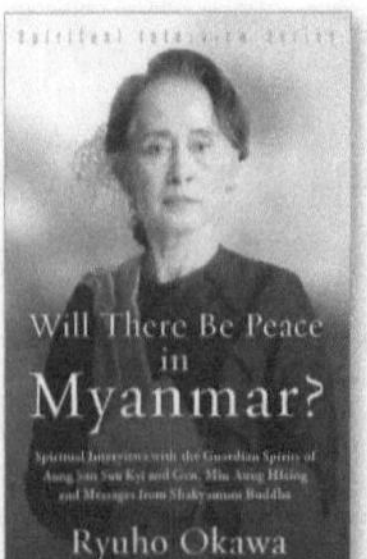

Will There Be Peace in Myanmar? (Tokyo: HS Press, 2021)

only provide disaster relief, then the country cannot be protected. Happy Science is expressing some hardline views, but you are doing so because it is necessary to alter such an attitude of Japan.

President Reagan called to stop the war on Earth and live in peace in case an alien threat comes from outer space. Ultimately, it is possible to make what he said come true, although we don't really want to do so. If we truly did, we would be doomed as an "eternal evil," so we want to avoid that.

6
Future Prospect of "Israel vs. Islam"

How to understand the Jewish god Yahweh

E

Let me ask you about a different subject. There is a country Israel, in the Middle East, and in recent years, there have been many conflicts between Iran and Israel as well. I think one of the problems is that people don't know very much about who Yahweh is. So, I would like to know how we should understand this god Yahweh from a religious point of view.

YAIDRON

I think what has appeared as Yahweh is an ethnic god. He represents the interest of Israelis and says that those who obey him will be praised, while those who disobey him will be punished. For Jewish people who originated from slaves, Yahweh is like their master.

However, it is true that Jewish people have a lot of intellectual heritage of humanity in their history. Christianity could become a very shallow religion if the Judaism aspects were completely omitted from it. Christianity is based on such a religion of the past, and even Jesus regarded himself as one of the teachers of Judaism.

But people cannot see this so-called god in heaven. Actually, "Yahweh" is another code name; many call themselves Yahweh, and you don't know who exactly is being referred to. This goes for Japanese religions as well. So, you should question if it is a single being who is using that name. There should also be ancestral gods in Israel, so they use that name a lot. I'm sure the being who has the aspect of the God of the Earth is also involved, as well as beings like us, who came from outer space. So, I think that no one had the brain to sort out the difference.

How Yaidron sees Moses, who represents Jewish people

E

What kinds of teachings did the beings from outer space send to the Jewish people? If there was any message on what they should do from the viewpoint of the universe, please tell us.

YAIDRON

It is often the case that at the roots of an ethnic group is a group of beings that had migrated from a different planet. For this reason, they all slightly differ in their ways of thinking. I think the Jewish people have such roots, although those from other planets also got mixed in as the ethnic group continued for a long time.

Moses represents the Jewish people, but from my perspective, he is... Hmm... Well, he is not the strong person everyone imagines him to be. In reality, he is a little more indecisive and is a roundabout person. He thinks in a way to detour things. Look at how he and his followers wandered in the desert for decades. If Moses was given the escape by calling the miracle from God to split the Red Sea, he could have immediately taken the land of Canaan and established a nation. Wandering the desert for decades sounds too odd. So, Moses himself was not a decisive person. To put it bluntly, in modern terms, Moses had a "masochistic" tendency.

Recently, Mandela of South Africa has been mentioned (as one of the soul siblings of Moses), but there is the question of whether a ninth-dimensional spirit should spend as long as 27 years in prison. This is too weak and too wasteful.

Nelson Mandela's Last Message to the World (Tokyo: HS Press, 2013)

Japan won against all Western countries except for the U.S. and helped India to become independent

YAIDRON

In India, too, people like Gandhi upheld nonresistance and took a roundabout way to achieve independence from the British, but they could not have achieved it with Gandhi's philosophy alone. In fact, it was very significant that Japan defeated Britain. There was a strong sense of inferiority among the Asian nations due to ethnic discrimination or racism. But after World War II, many countries gained independence because of Japan.

Back then, Japan defeated the British and also the French. Before that, Japan defeated Germany in World War I. There was the victory over Russia as well. Therefore, Japan beat every other white nation except for the U.S. Many Japanese people may depreciate themselves over this, but it is a fact that Japan had a victory over all nations except for the U.S.

China was defeated by Japan twice. The Qing Dynasty was a huge nation, which was called a sleeping lion, and it had the highest GDP in the world at that time. They were regarded as the U.S. today but were easily defeated by Japan and largely lagged behind. Since then, they created many movies depicting people trying to fight using kung fu and Shaolin martial art, but as these movies show, they lacked in modernity. But once China turned into a materialistic country, they are focusing on modernizing themselves based on materialism.

"Israel vs. Islam" will come to a conclusion within a decade

YAIDRON
Civilization experiments are mutually entangled in a complicated way. There are gods—or spiritual leaders, to be more specific—that protect specific races and others that move around different races. The world plan itself is complicated. Most of the part, history has been written as a result of the meetings of about 500 spirits, which is the same size as the Japanese Diet, or maybe more, with 500 to 1,000 spirits.

As for what to do with Israel and Islam, Ryuho Okawa, who has this gentle face, will decide in the end. Either of them will perish. This is not something we can decide on. El Cantare has the final say. Before that, we still have... well, maybe there won't even be 20 years left. In less than 20 years, or within a decade, I think it will come to a conclusion.

Yaidron sees that using Muhammad as a messenger means a shortage of talented people

E

God Thoth once said that since Israel is a democratic nation in the Middle East, it will be good if their worldview expands there (refer to *The Reason We Are Here*). On the other hand, even after numerous spiritual researches, we still don't know the real nature of the god Yahweh, who

The Reason We Are Here
(Tokyo: HS Press, 2020)

is said to be a jealous god or has a strong nature of an ethnic god. This doesn't necessarily mean that Allah is greater, but various beings spoke through Yahweh, among which was a being connected to the God of the Earth. Am I correct?

YAIDRON

In Judaism, there are also gods who are the equivalent of Japan's *tengu* (long-nosed goblins) or *yokai* (monsters and goblins).

It is also a mistake to think that Islam is ruled only by the God called Allah. They just use the name Allah, but it actually includes various kinds of spirits, many of which are ancestral spirits.

Another problem is that the true nature of jinn—an evil spirit of the desert areas—is also unknown. Just like the case of Allah, all kinds of evil and malicious spirits are referred to as "jinn." In the modern context, it appears in Disney's *Aladdin* as a giant in the magic lamp. Jinn can also use magic, so in a sense, he has a similar nature as Loki in the era of God Odin.

Therefore, in the center of the Arabian Peninsula, there are good and evil, as well as those that delude people.

There truly is the world of magic, and how to look at it is yet another issue. Everything is expressed as jinn, so we cannot tell who jinn actually is. We cannot tell who Allah is, either. Through the spiritual research of Happy Science, we just know that at least 40 spirits were involved in sending messages to create the Koran (refer to *My Lover, Cross the Valley of Tears*).

Muhammad himself did not have a strong spiritual power. And he was not literate and could not read. Imagine what would happen if spiritual messages were sent to someone who couldn't read or write. It's doubtful that he could make accurate judgments. This means a lot of descriptions were written by listening to the opinions of third parties. It clearly shows there was a lack of human resources to use a person who couldn't read or write as the only messenger of Allah or God. There was a severe lack of talent.

My Lover, Cross the Valley of Tears
(Happy Science, 2008)

The problems Yaidron sees in Islamic fundamentalism

YAIDRON

It is only natural for clashes to occur in the modern world if a religion founded in such a way follows the same pattern of behavior for 1,400 years as fundamentalists. In Japan, 1,400 years ago would be around the time of Prince Shotoku and a little before that—the era of the Asuka and Hakuho cultures. If you were told to do exactly the same things as people did back then, of course, many things cannot be done now. For example, you cannot pay your taxes with rice, labor, and cloth, or with kelp. This has to do with the change in the economic system, but fundamentalism has this aspect of sticking to the old practice.

Some parts of Islam have been westernized, like Turkey, but there are also those that engage in fundamentalist movements and try to go back to 1,400 years ago. The latter ignores women's rights, doesn't allow them to go to school, and has many wives as mistresses. Even Muhammad could be blamed if we were to raise the issue of human rights. After his first wife, Khadija—who was 15 years older than him—died in her 60s, he became engaged to a 6-year-old girl and started the married life with her when she was 9. In today's world, it would be a crime of deceiving and taking away a little girl, but it is considered acceptable according to fundamentalism.

You can also find a similar example in Japan. There is a story of Hikaru Genji nurturing a little girl for years, keeping her off of other men, and raising her to be the kind of woman he liked. Men have an instinct to want to do such a thing, but in terms of women's rights issues, this is severely problematic.

7
What Is Expected of Happy Science Now

Keep spreading the necessary knowledge and voicing strong opinions

A

Well, the time has come to end this session.

YAIDRON

[*To interviewer C*] Are you OK? Do you have anything else?

C

In closing, if there are things we can do or things you expect of us on Earth, please give us a message.

YAIDRON

Whether people will follow or not, I don't know, but people can act if they have the necessary knowledge. So, it is important to spread the necessary knowledge as widely as possible. It is a shame that the influence of Happy Science is not enough.

I understand there are many obstacles, but if you have become introverted and are only dealing with internal affairs, then you need to turn outward more. As for the international activities, you say that the teachings are spreading around the world, but in reality, you are satisfied with just securing a very small number of supporters. Even companies make progress, so religions must make even more progress with more enthusiasm and passion.

It is very rare for strong opinions to be voiced from Japan, so it is important to keep doing so. There are very few people in Japan who can say, "Save Hong Kong and Taiwan," for example. You need to say, "Save Myanmar from the military coup. The military regime is wrong, and Myanmar should return to a democratic country. China is pulling the strings behind the scenes," "Afghanistan also has China at the back. The Taliban is lying," or "China is just trying to complete the One Belt, One Road, so we must prevent the bad countries from arising and supporting it." China's ambition must be crushed.

From Japan, send messages on what America should do

YAIDRON

Unfortunately, Biden, who is so much like a Japanese, was chosen as the president of the U.S., and the course of history is beginning to change now. The bad situations we predicted are emerging now, so we have to urge Americans to become aware of this. From Japan, you must send messages on what America should do. Avoiding disputes may be a good thing for Japan that believes "harmony is to be valued," but sometimes it cannot be allowed.

The global economy will probably continue to be bad. It will be tough for you to navigate through the bad conditions.

Unless you increase the number of people who indirectly support Happy Science, you will become a minority group that upholds the idea that you alone are the chosen people, like Jewish elitism. That is not good. You need to become the majority.

C

Thank you very much.

YAIDRON

All right.

RYUHO OKAWA

[*Claps once.*] OK. That's all. It was quite long.

A

Thank you very much.

CHAPTER TWO

Tense Situation of Taiwan and Future Prospect of Coronavirus: UFO Reading 65 (Yaidron)

Originally recorded in Japanese on October 11, 2021 at the Special Lecture Hall of Happy Science in Japan and later translated into English.

It is said from ancient times that those who have attained enlightenment like Shakyamuni Buddha can use abilities beyond human knowledge freely at their will, namely the Six Divine Supernatural Powers (astral travel, spiritual sight, spiritual hearing, mind reading, fate reading, and extinction of worldly desires). These spiritual abilities of the highest level transcend the boundaries of time and space, and enable one to freely see through the past, present and future lives. Okawa is able to use these Six Divine Supernatural Powers freely and conduct various readings.

In this spiritual reading session, Okawa uses these abilities to conduct spiritual messages, spiritual vision, time-travel reading (seeing through the subject's past and future), remote viewing (sending part of the spirit body to a specific location and seeing the situation there), mind reading (reading the subject's thoughts and will, including those in a remote location), and mutual conversation (communicating with the thoughts of various beings that are beyond human contact).

The background of the recorded spiritual reading

On October 11, 2021, a UFO appeared in the sky. To investigate it, this reading was conducted on the spot.

In this chapter, the interviewer is symbolized as A.

1

Japan's Resolution Is Tested through Taiwan Crisis

The significance of the success of the movie, **The Laws of the Universe - The Age of Elohim**

RYUHO OKAWA

I think it's Mr. Yaidron. Is it you, Mr. Yaidron?

YAIDRON

Yes, it's Yaidron.

A

It's been a while.

Yaidron's UFO that appeared in the sky on October 11, 2021.

YAIDRON

Yes. Everyone is coming here right now.

A

Oh, I see.

YAIDRON

Several UFOs are gathering around.

A

Oh, that's right, there are more.

YAIDRON

More and more UFOs are coming. They are all gathering right now.

A

Thank you very much.

YAIDRON

You don't come out very often. Warm nights are rare.

A

Yes.

YAIDRON

It is such a blessing.

A

We had many cloudy and rainy days this year.

YAIDRON

Yes, indeed. The weather wasn't so great.

A

Right.

YAIDRON

(The movie) *The Laws of the Universe - The Age of Elohim* (Executive producer and original story: Ryuho Okawa, released in October 2021) has begun, and for the first week, it became No. 2 in theaters all over Japan and No. 1 at the box office in Shochiku Multiplex Theatres. I'm glad it is off to a good start.

A

Yes, thank you very much.

YAIDRON

We are happy too. I'm hoping it will be a hit. I hope that it will spread a little more to non-members (of Happy Science) this time.

A

Yes, that's right.

YAIDRON

Try to push harder. It is directly related to us.

A

Yes.

YAIDRON

The more it spreads, the closer we can get to Earth civilization, and it will be easier for us to come out and talk. But if people reject the movie, it means it's still too early for us, space beings, to come out.

Last year and this year too, the U.S. president acknowledged (the footage of alleged UFOs), and the gate to the universe is opening up a bit. So, in this current timing, I want you to make the movie a bit of a hit. Then people will want to know more and more about space, right? That is our hope.

If you say you can't, then I will say no more, but if you hope and want to be in touch with us, I'd like to give you all kinds of information. Nevertheless, I'll have to refrain from doing so if, by listening to my words, you start moving away from Earth's civilization or if people start to call you weird, eccentric, or crazy.

A

Yes.

YAIDRON

But since the U.S. acknowledged its existence, I don't think people will immediately call you "crazy." We put a bit of an effort into that, too, you know?

A

Oh, you did.

YAIDRON

Yes, we worked hard on making the U.S. admit it. We pressured them.

A

I see.

YAIDRON

Well, Japan is submissive to foreign countries. For now, I want people to understand the work we're doing a little more.

A

Indeed.

YAIDRON

We are doing important work.

A

Yes.

The three-step strategy of Xi Jinping

YAIDRON

I'll answer anything you want to ask since it's been a while. If you don't have anything, I'll speak. Do you have anything?

A

Well, in August you did a lot...

YAIDRON

Yes.

R. A. Goal's Words for the Future (Tokyo: HS Press, 2021)

Spiritual Messages from Metatron: Light in the Times of Crisis (Tokyo: HS Press, 2021)

A

You were helping a lot with Master's work. You, Mr. Yaidron, Mr. Metatron...

YAIDRON

Right.

A

And also Mr. R. A. Goal.

YAIDRON

Yes. We are all involved in *The Laws Of Messiah*.

A

Yes, starting with *The Laws Of Messiah*...

YAIDRON

The next year's main book.

The Laws Of Messiah
(New York: IRH Press, 2022)

A

And right now, Taiwan's situation is not so good.

YAIDRON

Yes, it's true. There's a crisis on the horizon.

A

We have our branch manager (in Taiwan).

YAIDRON

Yes, right. But it's the biggest crisis ever.

A

I'm sure they (the people of Taiwan) are feeling the danger.

YAIDRON

Hmm. Yes, it is probably the biggest crisis ever in 40 years, since the Tiananmen Square incident.

A

How do you see the situation?

YAIDRON

Well, right now, mainland China is threatening Taiwan by operating landing drills in Fujian and showing them on TV. Basically, Xi Jinping's main goal is to win without fighting, using the Art of War by Sun Tzu. His ultimate goal is to threaten Taiwan to the point they feel too despaired of fighting, disarm themselves and accept the "one country, two systems" policy. Of course, he doesn't want any damage to China either.

His second strategy is to significantly strengthen the Chinese military to convince Taiwan that they have no hope of winning, no matter what. Even if their allies do come, by the time they arrive, it would be too late. Creating such a big gap of military strength is their aim. This second strategy is for 2025, but they actually want to make a helpless situation for Taiwan before then.

The third step is to aim for a complete reversal of power with the U.S. by 2030, so that China can go ahead doing whatever they want toward any country, completely ignoring the opinions of the world. Xi Jinping wants to go that far during his lifetime presidency.

A

I see.

YAIDRON

These are his three-step strategy.

China will shake Taiwan and Japan

YAIDRON

At the moment, China is putting pressure on Taiwan. They also send a lot of spies to instigate the protest movement to drive Tsai Ing-wen into a corner.

A

I see.

YAIDRON

Taiwan and China are very near to each other.

A

Yes.

YAIDRON

Fujian and Taiwan are so close that both will suffer tremendous damage should missiles be fired at each other.

Taiwan also has an army of over 500,000 soldiers. Even if China amasses the military in Fujian, Taiwan is now increasing its missile production and is even building long-range missiles. Taiwan's government has ordered the production of more missiles. Making long-range missiles means Taiwan is not only looking at Fujian but also planning to shoot Beijing.

A

I see.

YAIDRON

Yes, that's what it means, right? Taiwan is rushing it. That's why China wants to put pressure on Tsai Ing-wen at an earlier time. But the opinion of the world is different. After seeing how Hong Kong ended up, people of the world can see how Taiwan will be like under China. The world already knows that the "one country, two systems" is an obvious lie.

A

That's right.

YAIDRON

Even NHK (Japan's public broadcaster) is starting to say that China's revolution is wrong. As Hannah Arendt said, the purpose of revolution is the foundation of freedom. Stealing people's freedom is not a revolution, but it's oppression, tyranny, a return to the imperial system. In reality, China only has an imperial system now.

A

Yes.

YAIDRON

China created an imperial system in the name of the Communist Party. But I'm sure the global public opinion will put a lot of pressure on them.

China is watching carefully how weak Biden is, and also how (Prime Minister) Kishida of Japan will...

A

That's right.

YAIDRON

China is watching how they will react. Now, China is applying pressure by sending Chinese military jets into (Taiwan's) Air Defense Identification Zone. At most, more than 50 jets a day. I'm sure the same will happen around the Senkaku Islands. They'll try to shake Taiwan and Japan to see how strong their resolution is.

A

Hmm.

YAIDRON

Japan is slow to react to this matter. Kishida is another liberal person. He takes things too easy and insists that nuclear weapons should be eliminated from the world. He says such a thing, even when North Korea has been developing hydrogen bombs.

China is probably not afraid of Japan at all, but I'm sure they'll send a few signals. For example, they may conduct armed or threatening reconnaissance against the Senkaku Islands. I think there's a possibility that China will hit a minor "jab" at Taiwan and see if Japan's public opinion will turn around.

Now you have (the movie) *The Laws of the Universe - The Age of Elohim*, and the next (movie) is *The Cherry Bushido* (Executive producer and original story: Ryuho Okawa, scheduled to be released in 2022). I think this tension will grow even more toward the year-end and New Year holidays.

Can North Korean and Chinese missiles be intercepted?

A

There has been a rumor that North Korea's Kim Jong-un is recently using a body double.

YAIDRON

Yes, but it's hard to say. It is said that there are more than 10 body doubles, though. It's true he is afraid of being assassinated.

A

I see.

YAIDRON

He also has been turning his sister (Kim Yo-jong) into an authority figure. Well, he's managed to be in power for over 10 years now.

A

Yes, that's true.

YAIDRON

Well, North Korea really did develop atomic and hydrogen bombs... And now they created missiles that Japan can't defend itself against. I mean, their new cruise missiles can fly up and down and can't be shot down with Japan's PAC-3 interceptors.

China is also developing missiles that can penetrate an aircraft carrier. That, too, will be hard to cope with. Especially the ones that fly out of the stratosphere and then fall—I think China definitely has it, and it's said that North Korea might have it, too. The missile that goes out of the stratosphere then falls has a very fast fall speed. If it is aimed right, no missile can shoot it down because it falls at Mach 20. It is fast, way too fast. It's too fast to shoot down. It can't be helped.

Therefore, if we are to stop it, we will do so before it launches. I'm sure the U.S. is wiretapping them, so when the command for such an attack is issued, they will most probably launch some kind of preemptive strike, as I don't think they are that stupid. It's not that the U.S. act with just Biden's say. His approval will certainly be necessary, but their military is always vigilant.

After what happened at the military withdrawal from Afghanistan, the U.S. is now saying they will withdraw their troops from Iraq next within this year. It would truly be embarrassing if the situation turns out like Afghanistan, but their purpose of withdrawing troops is to gather forces in the Far East. The Far East is covered mainly by the Seventh Fleet, and the Fifth Fleet is in the Middle East. So, they are currently trying to pull out the Fifth Fleet from the Middle East and focus on the Far East to prepare for any contingency.

A

I see.

YAIDRON

So, if China takes it as a mere weakness of the U.S., they are mistaken. The U.S. plans to join the Fifth and Seventh Fleets to be ready.

And now, Australia and Canada have also sent warships, and so has the U.K. Even Germany, which used to have the largest trade with China, is taking a tough stance.

A

I understand.

YAIDRON

Right now, there is a fight over the Trans-Pacific Partnership (TPP) issue. If the TPP members let Taiwan in and not China, they (China) will probably go ballistic like gangsters. They will threaten and shake the members as if saying, "Do you think your country can survive by keeping off the world's greatest power?" There will be a battle over whether such a threat will lead to China's international isolation or other countries succumbing to China's intimidation.

2
The Timing of Taiwan's First Crisis

What will happen to China's domestic economy

A

It seems that a major Chinese real estate developer is on the verge of bankruptcy.

YAIDRON

Yes, it is. It's in deficit. Well, it's a big issue; ¥33 trillion (about US$300 billion) in debt is pretty large.

A

It is large.

YAIDRON

The company can't survive any longer. But it's not completely a private company. The government seems to be trying to give it a soft landing, as it's not completely private. This industry is starting to crumble economically.

And China's domestic economy is also stalling, and the economic condition is getting worse. They are trying to show that it will get better, but it's obvious that it's not going to happen.

China is using companies equivalent to Google and Facebook to monitor people. But such companies like Google and Facebook are now in a difficult position. It has become like a battle between the state versus information technology companies. Well, they have been doing two-way diplomacy, but they now have to make up their mind on their "home country." Stateless global companies have to decide their home country.

Well, you never know what might happen. I can't say for sure at this point, but my prediction is that the first crisis will occur... It's October now. So, I think the first shakeup will occur between now and around March.

A

By China?

YAIDRON

Yes. They will make the first move to shake Taiwan. They will know how serious Taiwan is by seeing their reaction, and at the same time, they will see how other countries in the world will move. I think they will test it and throw the dice. Xi Jinping himself has boastfully declared that he will make "one China" while he is in power.

I think your movie contains that kind of message, so I want as many people as possible to see it. I think it was worth making it.

The current Japanese political situation amid the approaching crisis

YAIDRON

Well, what should we do with Japan? I'm having a bit of trouble because Japan is slow. The next election is coming up, so depending on the results, things may change again. Hawkish people...

RYUHO OKAWA

Oh, will it (UFO) be out of sight soon?

A

It's still on the screen.

RYUHO OKAWA

Is it OK?

A

It's shining.

YAIDRON

Hawkish people seemed to support Ms. Takaichi. But there is a possibility that China may belittle her because she is a woman. Things are delicate and difficult. Kishida is now more under the control of Abe and Aso than what people thought. So, I don't think Kishida will make a big change.

Anyway, the economy is the key. The coronavirus cases are slightly decreasing in Japan now, so it's necessary to revive the economy and at the same time strengthen the defense system. Also, natural disasters are likely to occur, so I'm sure a crisis management system would be established to cope with them.

It's an ordeal, indeed. Can Kishida get past the deep water of the election? Can he overcome the Taiwan crisis after that? Japan has sent out a message of support for Taiwan but is it just emotional support, or is it more than that? I think China wants to know about that, so they will test Japan.

Another issue is missile launches from submarines. China, North Korea, and also South Korea now have the ability to launch missiles from submarines. Thinking about the future, the Far East will be in an emergency... Russia is also capable of launching missiles from submarines. Since four countries now have launch capabilities, it will be dangerous in case of the Far East emergency.

RYUHO OKAWA
Oh, maybe the UFO hid behind the clouds.

A
It's still slightly shining.

RYUHO OKAWA
All right, well, we can still talk.

YAIDRON
You need to be resolute. What can the Happiness Realization Party do? It is a really tough, tough fight.

All the other parties are the same, right? They just talk about compensation for coronavirus and dole-out policies. It's all about that.

A

They are still under materialistic values.

YAIDRON

That's all there is. They still can't put the issue of China into the campaign goals... Hmm so, they do not push the issue of defending Taiwan or the Hong Kong issue to the forefront in their campaign.

A

Not at all, I think.

YAIDRON

It's obvious. At most, they may say something like, "We will pay attention to that issue." Well, I wonder if Japan can last as a country.

A

That's the concern.

YAIDRON

When there is Taiwan crisis, I think the Senkaku Islands and Okinawa crises are also around the corner. I'm sure these crises will come. I don't think it will take so much time.

A

Even though the people of Ishigaki Island applied to put a sign on Senkaku, the government rejected their application.

YAIDRON

Well [*smiles wryly*], when the government refuses to put up a sign that says, "Ishigaki City, Okinawa Prefecture," that is the same as not recognizing it as Japan's territory.

A

I understand if the government does it instead of the people of Ishigaki Island.

YAIDRON

They are afraid that it may provoke China's accusation. Well, basically, it is the same as being scared of the gangsters, right?

A

Well, yes.

YAIDRON

It's like putting up a sign that says, "No gangsters allowed." They fear that it might infuriate the *yakuza*, right?

A

Their stance is: "Far from Jupiter, far from his thunder."

YAIDRON

The Komeito party is also involved in this matter, I think. Japan's Ministry of Land, Infrastructure, Transport, and Tourism has been under the control of Komeito for a long time. Well, I myself...

Tsai Ing-wen intends to defend Taiwan, and she is even building missiles. Japan is also slowly building long-range missiles, but this is the country where we don't know what and by when it will do. Nothing is clear about it, partly due to information control.

What China will do next after the first coronavirus war

A

Are there space people who are supporting Ms. Tsai Ing-wen?

YAIDRON

Of course, there are.

A

Of course?

YAIDRON

Yes, of course. I'm looking at Taiwan objectively, but I'm willing to protect it when I have to. So, maybe something will happen. I'm thinking of causing something, but I am wondering in what form would people be the happiest.

China's attack won't be over in just one time; for Taiwan, it's like the Mongol invasions of Japan. Even if they dodge the first attack, it's not the end. China will get more and more desperate to fight because if China continues to lose, there will be uprisings in Tibet, Mongolia, and the Uyghur region. There are already many insurgents in the country. It has been exposed internationally that they have too much of a bad reputation now.

A

In an NHK program featuring China, a Chinese-American person said, "After all, China has always been a country of imperial rule."

YAIDRON

Yes, that is exactly right.

A

That person said, "Xi Jinping is trying to do the same."

YAIDRON

Yes, yes.

A

That is what was being said. It means that China has always been such a country, right?

YAIDRON

In a sense, to put it the other way around, they claim by looking at China's history, "What is wrong with the imperial rule?"

A

Exactly.

YAIDRON

They are saying, "We have been chosen as new emperors, so we are trying to unify the whole nation and the world."

A

Yes. Can that be changed, though?

YAIDRON

I don't know. But they did when it was the old dynasty of Qin. When the nation "China" seized as far as Europe a long time ago, it even dominated Judea, now called Israel.

A

Oh, yes.

YAIDRON

It's true. There is such a history in the past. So, expansion is a virtue (for China). Repelling different ethnic groups is good too. It is good to dominate. They have such ideologies. In short, there is no such idea as "love that gives." "Love that takes" is good for them. It is good to expand.

The population can be the bulwark for a nuclear war. This is the reason why China is stating a bigger number of populations, but in reality, their population is starting to decrease slightly.

Now that the first coronavirus war is settling down a little, I think they are thinking about what to do next.

A

Why is the pandemic settling down?

YAIDRON

It's because China is no longer actively spreading the virus.

A

Oh, right, I see.

YAIDRON
Evidence will be found if they do it now. They were spreading the virus in the beginning, when people were not aware. But they are no longer actively spreading the virus.

Coronavirus will die out gradually if it is not supplied; it is not immortal. The period the virus can rage is short. The virus spreads when there is a lot of prey, but it can't live long.

The second attack may not be by coronavirus. China might seize Taiwan while they put other areas in chaos. That's one way. I think they will try to distract people's attention from Taiwan. They are already doing such plotting all over the world.

Their greatest success was the Biden presidency. When Biden was still the vice president of the Obama administration, they already took in Biden's son by making him a Chinese-related company board member and putting him in a sticky situation. However, the U.S. won't keep silent if new national interest issues arise. Then, Biden may contrarily turn militant to pretend as if his relationship with China is a false accusation. This, too, is possible.

Recently, a military regime was established in many countries in quick succession, so indeed, it's a dangerous situation. The world is extremely dangerous. It will be hard for the U.S. to handle if terrorism and wars occur simultaneously in various areas. One concern is the withdrawal of the U.S. troops from Iraq at the end of this year. If something similar to what happened in Afghanistan occurs, they will lose their self-confidence.

A

You mean the U.S.

YAIDRON

This is a point to watch out for.

The international community knows that China is behind the coup in Myanmar, but they can't intervene because there is no clear evidence. It's absolutely clear that China is supporting the military. This is a tug of war. Can Europe, the U.S., Australia, and Japan be united? Is it really possible that the TPP allows Taiwan to join and block the Beijing government? These issues can be the judging points.

A

I see. I definitely don't want China to join TPP.

YAIDRON

Well, China is obviously disliked by other nations.

A

I mean, their ideas toward the economy are different in the first place.

Ah, the UFO might disappear soon.

RYUHO OKAWA

Oh, it might disappear.

3

The Idea of Justice the World Needs Now

It is about what to choose according to the values of the Earth

YAIDRON

Is there anything else you want to ask?

A

This may completely change the topic. I think this is the same for Xi Jinping and Kim Jong-un, but they became somewhat strong. When they become strong, and their power as a person increases... I think Mr. Yaidron and other space beings are great existences, but at the same time, you have faith in the Creator, and you believe in Him.

YAIDRON

Yes.

A

How can you stay connected to God without losing faith, without being conceited, or without trying to attract people's faith in you? What kind of mind makes it possible to be that way?

YAIDRON

This is quite a different topic. I need to talk about a much longer history of the universe to answer your question. It is not that easy. What has been revealed so far is not enough. It is a much longer story. Well, we are tied with a much stronger bond. Most of the knowledge you have now is about the history of just recent 2,000 to 3,000 years, and you don't have a clue about the history of 10,000 years.

A

What advice can you give to ordinary people then?

YAIDRON

El Cantare is the God of the Earth. At the same time, however, He is beyond the God of the Earth. He has been involved in various battles for justice and arbitrations in different galaxies. At such times, we worked together with Him. In the end, it is about what to choose according to the values of the Earth. If we can't make judgments ourselves, we will follow El Cantare's decision. We will take it as the judgment of the Earth and act based on it.

China has been shaken economically now. It is shaken by international isolation too. Also, we are trying to induce an uprising inside China, while trying to increase the number of nations that support Taiwan. But should an undiscriminating massacre occur while people of the world are watching on TV, we will take some action to inflict some damage to China, with permission from El Cantare. We have various weapons; if the damage is caused by the weapon not of the Earth, people won't understand what has happened.

A

I see. Before that, however, (Japanese) people need to have a strong determination to protect their own nation by themselves.

YAIDRON

Of course, they should do that.

A

Japanese people must learn to have a perspective of justice, right?

YAIDRON

As I have been telling you repeatedly, Japan must decide clearly that it will fight under Western values and join hands with nations such as Taiwan, India and Australia to reject the Chinese ancient and outdated values. If they do, the world will then move in that direction, I think. But it would be dangerous if Japan were to be taken in by China easily.

A

That's right.

YAIDRON

China is trying to take in Russia as well. Like President Reagan, we may need to call Russia, North Korea, China, and Iran the "axis of evil."

Other reforms needed in addition to Chinese reformation

YAIDRON

It can't be helped that Islam will also have damage. Islamic people are not united. They don't have any thoughts to protect Islam at all. All they do is fight between different sects, so it cannot be helped. They are all terrible.

A

That's right. Despite the fact that they share the same faith, there have been many wars among them.

YAIDRON

Some reform is necessary. The world trend after the Gulf War is actually intended to... We are also thinking of reforming Islam. We are trying to let people know that it's not good to backlash and move toward restoring the old-style imperial rule.

These two things will finally happen. I think that the Middle East issue—reformation of Islam—and reformation of China will both take place, while El Cantare is still on earth. We will finish the game.

A

Yes.

YAIDRON

If Xi Jinping managed to serve until 2030, that would be impressive, but he may not last easily till then. Either way, he will be frightened if the U.S. says it will fire long-range ballistic missiles into Beijing. He doesn't think China can win a war on its own. The U.S. is much stronger. The performance of their weapons is much better than that of China.

Xi Jinping's strategy is to pressure the U.S. to withdraw all its bases in Okinawa, Guam, and Hawaii. So, at some point in time...

If this situation is still the same in 2024, Mr. Trump may still have a chance.

A

I see.

YAIDRON

We won't abandon you.

A

Thank you so much.

YAIDRON

We will protect nations with faith, and at the same time, we are trying to let various faiths compete and purify them. Although this movement of the Savior from Japan may still seem small now, we believe that it will definitely turn into a huge power.

A

Thank you very much.

Today's Yaidron's UFO

A

Today's session is a UFO reading, so may I ask...

YAIDRON

UFO reading, yes.

A

What is the shape of your UFO?

YAIDRON

Today's one is about 70 meters (about 230 feet) long.

A

It's huge.

YAIDRON

It is big. We are on a rather large UFO, well, maybe a medium-sized one. If it is for surveillance, the sizing of around 20 meters (about 65 feet) is enough, but this one is about 70 meters.

The clouds are a little scattered right now, but a few other UFOs came with us. When we started talking, they came in quickly.

So, our UFO is about 70 meters long, and it is equipped with some defense systems. Even if the aliens related to the one called "Bazooka" abruptly come to bother us, we'll be able to fight them.

A

How many passengers can board your UFO?

YAIDRON

About 30 people are on board now.

A

Including both men and women?

YAIDRON

Yes. About five of them are women.

A

I see.

YAIDRON

The 30-crew fighter jet may seem small, but our UFO of this size alone can destroy a whole country. There is such a difference in the level of science and technology.

A

I understand.

YAIDRON

We are strong, really. So, we have to target that chance. We have to aim for a good chance.

4

Forecast of the World after the Coronavirus Pandemic

China's next aim

YAIDRON

Coronavirus has caused damage to the world, but if China is left exempt from their responsibility, I cannot forgive that.

A

That is the point.

YAIDRON

If they do something even worse, it's time for them to be punished.

A

Oh, what about anthrax?

YAIDRON

I think they are preparing it.

A

So, they are preparing it.

YAIDRON

Yes, I think so. They aim to cause chaos.

A

Oh. So, they are planning to control the world while causing chaos.

YAIDRON

Yes, yes. Europe and the U.S. are basically their targets, and Australia has become unbearable for them nowadays. I think they are targeting that area.

A

I see.

YAIDRON

Well, it was good of you to have sent out the information. Yes, they are definitely targeting there. If they truly make a military invasion next time, they need to cause chaos in other parts of the world. Of course, Japan could also be a target. However, anthrax won't spread like coronavirus, so only people in the targeted area will die. That is how it's going to be like.

A

I see. We have to be careful.

YAIDRON

They will likely cause a serious incident and create confusion. They will hint at their involvement while insisting that they didn't do it. In this way, they will try to make things obscure. Their number-one priority is to frighten people.

A

How do you see the future of the coronavirus? Will it continue to spread?

YAIDRON

Yes, it will still go on. The whole world is watching over China, so I think it's getting a little difficult for them to scatter, but they still have the virus. So, I guess they are thinking of another way.

A

I see.

YAIDRON

For example, they may think about an aerial spray type. It's getting a little difficult to carry the virus into other countries, so an airborne dispersal or something like that is possible.

Also, the Winter Olympics are coming up in February next year in Beijing. They don't want to lose face, so they are thinking about what to do next, considering the position as a host country.

I think they are hoping that Taiwan will surrender by then. So, the pressure will continue for the rest of the year.

A

A country that is going to hold a peace festival is...

YAIDRON

Yes. Doing wars.

A

Doing things like massacring the Uyghurs and threatening Hong Kong and Taiwan. It is like, "How are you even able to hold a peace festival?"

YAIDRON

Yes, indeed. It's been called the Genocide Olympics.

A

Yes, truly. I understand.

YAIDRON

That's their ambition, but we have to think about how to counteract it. Happy Science International Headquarters does not have much power as it appears. It is unfortunate they don't have enough power to influence other countries yet. It's too bad.

Japan itself should be prepared for China's ambition.

What people on earth have to work on

YAIDRON

Nevertheless, even Mr. Kishida, who is a liberal, has said things like missile defense, a preemptive strike against the enemy, and support for Taiwan, so I think 12 years of your activities (by founding Happiness Realization Party) were not in vain. Eventually, your efforts will be acknowledged.

A

Even so, it's important to continue spreading the messages of Master Okawa, beings in the universe, and the guiding spirits in the heavenly world.

YAIDRON

Yes. I will—not just I but—we will appear in the final stage and ask for El Cantare's judgment. We will take it as the judgment of the Earth and take action when necessary.

A

Yes.

YAIDRON

But please be noted that what we are going to do could be fiercer than an atomic or hydrogen bomb, though in a different form. I won't say what it will look like, but I will show you how powerful we are. Well, I think it will happen in the not-too-distant future.

A

I see.

YAIDRON

I could say a little clearer, but I also want to see how China will move since they are acting provocatively now.

A

Yes. Also, the people on earth have to...

YAIDRON

You have to make an effort.

A

Yes. There are things to do.

YAIDRON

You are not successful in elections, but you are sending out messages through movies and other media, as well as publishing books.

A

Yes, but I believe it is also important for the Happiness Realization Party to deliver messages. The election itself is not our aim. We have to change the country, and we have to spread God's name.

YAIDRON

Yes, that is right.

But there still is the crisis. It's a bit troublesome that the prime minister is from Hiroshima. It would be good if the enemy were to discard their atomic bombs by the "No More Hiroshima" statement, but it would make no sense if our allies got rid of it.

I believe you should be persistent and say what needs to be said.

A

Yes. Well, I'm very grateful to have talked to you today after a long time.

YAIDRON

Yes. Well, I heard you saying that space beings are not coming even though (the movie) *The Laws of the Universe* is showing. So, I came.

A

But you've been helping us in many ways behind the scenes, including work related to *The Laws Of Messiah*.

China's logic behind the movement to eliminate CO_2

YAIDRON

Ms. Tsai Ing-wen was very happy when Master Ryuho Okawa visited Taiwan and said (in the lecture), "This time, Japan will not forsake Taiwan" (refer to *Love for the Future*). She was very happy, yes.

A

Yes, it had a great impact.

YAIDRON

It showed the determination not to back down this time.

A

Yes, that's right.

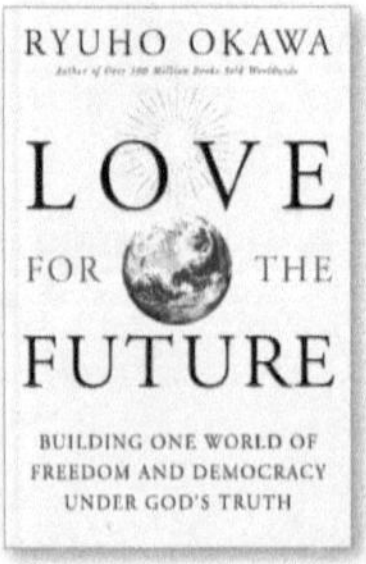

Love for the Future
(New York: IRH Press, 2019)

YAIDRON

Using the movement to eliminate CO_2, China is trying to make the world believe that oil is no longer necessary, so there is no need to protect the sea lanes. They actually take advantage of "Greta religion."

A

Yes.

YAIDRON

If we shift to a civilization that doesn't use oil anymore, we won't need tankers to transport it. If sea lanes are not needed, there will be no need to protect the Taiwan Strait. This is their logic. But I don't think that's going to happen.

A

China is experiencing electricity shortages now, right?

YAIDRON

Yes, blackouts are still going on, so as a civilized country or industrialized country, they have already reached their limits. In countries like that, the statistics are inaccurate, so people don't know.

A

This is often taught for the individuals, but when a country gains power, it should also become public.

YAIDRON

That's right. They are far from that as they are. It is like the land of the Vikings. They really are just pirates.

A

I see.

YAIDRON

I think it is necessary to let them know that without friendly relations with the international community, there will be no development.

Of course, the people inside are heavily brainwashed and controlled by the Communist Party. But among the Communist Party that has less than 100 million members, there are some insurgents. So, it's important to let them know how much damage they could suffer. Xi Jinping is trying to brainwash them, but if they think about the pros and cons of following the brainwash, and the answer is full of cons, then they will definitely change their ideas.

We will take action in some way or another.

A

Yes.

YAIDRON

Well, if I say it too clearly, it may cause you trouble, so that's all I can say.

A

Yes. OK, let's wrap up today's session.

YAIDRON

Yes, thank you.

A

Thank you very much.

RYUHO OKAWA

[*Claps twice.*]

Afterword

There is something called the Bell Theory: The big bell of a temple will not be moved by a single push with your finger, but if you keep pushing it with an appropriate rhythm, again and again, even with such little power, the bell will gradually start swinging in a large motion. In the same way, if you keep voicing your opinions, no matter how small your voice may be, they will eventually start to influence the world. These are the words of the late Prof. Shoichi Watanabe. He said this as words of self-discipline and as words of hope. Inspired also by these words, I have been fighting against the common sense of the world, fair and square, for more than 35 years.

So far, I have given more than 3,350 lectures, published over 2,900 books, and created over 23 movies. My books have been translated into 37 languages, and we have believers across 164 countries. Even so, the world does not change right away, and people are living in communal fantasy.

The God of the Earth has already spoken. His words surpass Judaism, Buddhism, Christianity, Islam, and Hinduism of the past. It is your Power of Believing that will make the bell swing in a big motion.

Ryuho Okawa
Master & CEO of Happy Science Group
October 19, 2021

For a deeper understanding of Spiritual Messages from Yaidron: Save the World from Destruction, *see other books below by Ryuho Okawa:*

· *Love for the Future* (New York: IRH Press, 2019)
· *Inside the Mind of President Biden* (Tokyo: HS Press, 2021)
· *Will There Be Peace in Myanmar?* (Tokyo: HS Press, 2021)
· *Nelson Mandela's Last Message to the World* (Tokyo: HS Press, 2013)
· *The Reason We Are Here* (Tokyo: HS Press, 2020)
· *Spiritual Messages from Metatron: Light in the Times of Crisis* (Tokyo: HS Press, 2021)
· *R. A. Goal's Words for the Future* (Tokyo: HS Press, 2021)

The following book is only available at Happy Science locations. Please see the contact information on pp. 176-177.

· *My Lover, Cross the Valley of Tears* (Happy Science, 2008)

ABOUT THE AUTHOR

RYUHO OKAWA was born on July 7th 1956, in Tokushima, Japan. After graduating from the University of Tokyo with a law degree, he joined a Tokyo-based trading house. While working at its New York headquarters, he studied international finance at the Graduate Center of the City University of New York. In 1981, he attained Great Enlightenment and became aware that he is El Cantare with a mission to bring salvation to all humankind. In 1986, he established Happy Science. It now has members in over 160 countries across the world, with more than 700 branches and temples as well as 10,000 missionary houses around the world. The total number of lectures has exceeded 3,350 (of which more than 150 are in English) and over 2,900 books (of which more than 600 are Spiritual Interview Series) have been published, many of which are translated into 37 languages. Many of the books, including *The Laws of the Sun* have become best sellers or million sellers. To date, Happy Science has produced 24 movies. The original story and original concept were given by the Executive Producer Ryuho Okawa. Recent movie titles are *Into the Dreams...and Horror Experiences* (live-action, August 2021), *The Laws of the Universe-The Age of Elohim* (animation movie, October 2021), *The Cherry Bushido* (live-action movie scheduled to be released in February 2022). He has also composed the lyrics and music of over 450 songs, such as theme songs and featured songs of movies. Moreover, he is the Founder of Happy Science University and Happy Science Academy (Junior and Senior High School), Founder and President of the Happiness Realization Party, Founder and Honorary Headmaster of Happy Science Institute of Government and Management, Founder of IRH Press Co., Ltd., and the Chairperson of NEW STAR PRODUCTION Co., Ltd. and ARI Production Co., Ltd.

WHAT IS EL CANTARE?

The God of the Earth El Cantare is the Primordial God of Earth's spirit group. He is the supreme existence whom Jesus called Father, and is *Ame-no-Mioya-Gami*, Japanese Father God. El Cantare has sent down his branch spirits, such as Shakyamuni Buddha and Hermes, many times to guide humankind and develop many civilizations. Currently, the core consciousness of El Cantare has descended to Earth as Master Ryuho Okawa, and is giving teachings to unite various religions and to integrate various fields of study to guide all humankind to true happiness.

Alpha is a part of the core consciousness of El Cantare who descended to Earth around 330 million years ago. Alpha preached Earth's Truths to harmonize and unify Earth-born humans and space people who came from other planets.

Elohim is a part of El Cantare's core consciousness who descended to Earth around 150 million years ago. He gave wisdom, mainly on the differences of light and darkness, good and evil.

Ame-no-Mioya-Gami (Japanese Father God) is the Creator God and the original ancestor of the Japanese people who appears in the ancient literature, *Hotsuma Tsutae*. It is believed that He descended on the foothills of Mt. Fuji about 30,000 years ago and built the Fuji dynasty, which is the root of the Japanese civilization. With justice as the central pillar, Ame-no-Mioya-Gami's teachings spread to ancient civilizations of other countries in the world.

Shakyamuni Buddha was born as a prince into the Shakya Clan in India around 2,600 years ago. When he was 29 years old, he renounced the world and sought enlightenment. He later attained Great Enlightenment and founded Buddhism.

Hermes is one of the 12 Olympian gods in Greek mythology, but the spiritual Truth is that he taught the teachings of love and progress around 4,300 years ago that became the origin of the current Western civilization. He is a hero that truly existed.

Ophealis was born in Greece around 6,500 years ago and was the leader who took an expedition to as far as Egypt. He is the God of miracles, prosperity, and arts, and is known as Osiris in the Egyptian mythology.

Rient Arl Croud was born as a king of the ancient Incan Empire around 7,000 years ago and taught about the mysteries of the mind. In the heavenly world, he is responsible for the interactions that take place between various planets.

Thoth was an almighty leader who built the golden age of the Atlantic civilization around 12,000 years ago. In the Egyptian mythology, he is known as god Thoth.

Ra Mu was a leader who built the golden age of the civilization of Mu around 17,000 years ago. As a religious leader and a politician, he ruled by uniting religion and politics.

WHAT IS A SPIRITUAL MESSAGE?

We are all spiritual beings living on this earth. The following is the mechanism behind Master Ryuho Okawa's spiritual messages.

1 You are a spirit

People are born into this world to gain wisdom through various experiences and return to the other world when their lives end. We are all spirits and repeat this cycle in order to refine our souls.

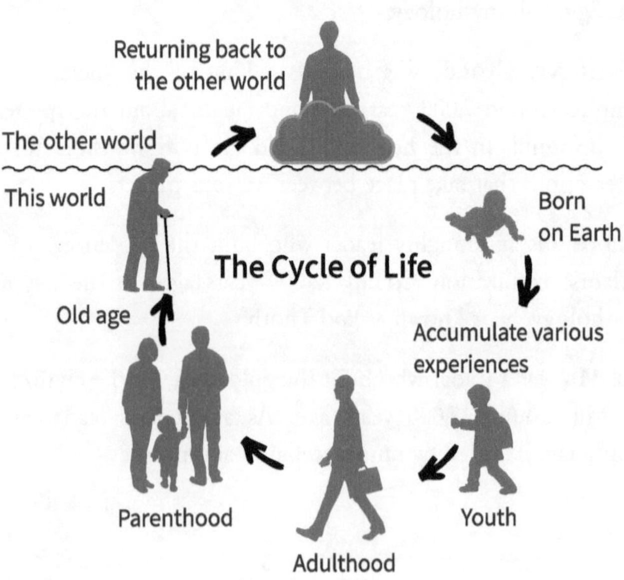

2 You have a guardian spirit

Guardian spirits are those who protect the people who are living on this earth. Each of us has a guardian spirit that watches over us and guides us from the other world. They were us in our past life, and are identical in how we think.

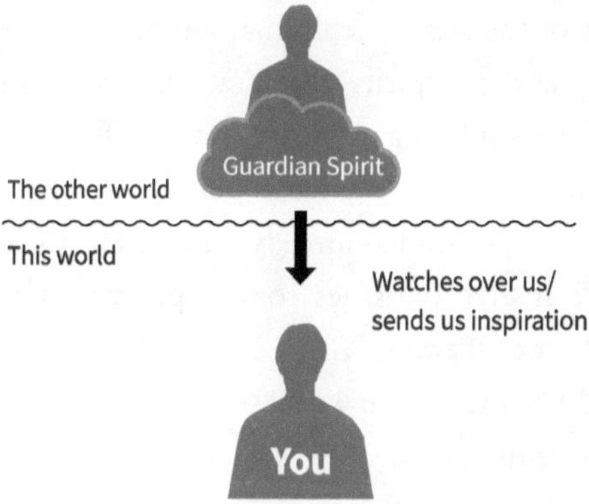

3 How spiritual messages work

Master Ryuho Okawa, through his enlightenment, is capable of summoning any spirit from anywhere in the world, including the spirit world.

Master Okawa's way of receiving spiritual messages is fundamentally different from that of other psychic mediums who undergo trances and are thereby completely taken over by the spirits they are channeling.

Master Okawa's attainment of a high level of enlightenment enables him to retain full control of his consciousness and body throughout the duration of the spiritual message. To allow the spirits to express their own thoughts and personalities freely, however, Master Okawa usually softens the dominancy of his consciousness. This way, he is able to keep his own philosophies out of the way and ensure that the spiritual messages are pure expressions of the spirits he is channeling.

Since guardian spirits think at the same subconscious level as the person living on earth, Master Okawa can summon the spirit and find out what the person on earth is actually thinking. If the person has already returned to the other world, the spirit can give messages to the people living on earth through Master Okawa.

Since 2009, more than 1,200 sessions of spiritual messages have been openly recorded by Master Okawa, and the majority of these have been published. Spiritual messages from the guardian spirits of people living today such as Donald Trump, former Japanese Prime Minister Shinzo Abe and Chinese President Xi Jinping, as well as spiritual messages sent from the spirit world by Jesus Christ, Muhammad, Thomas Edison, Mother Teresa, Steve Jobs and Nelson Mandela are just a tiny pack of spiritual messages that were published so far.

Domestically, in Japan, these spiritual messages are being read by a wide range of politicians and mass media, and the high-level contents of these books are delivering an impact even more on politics, news and public opinion. In recent years, there have been spiritual messages recorded in English, and English translations are being done on the spiritual messages given in Japanese. These have been published overseas, one after another, and have started to shake the world.

For more about spiritual messages and a complete list of books in the Spiritual Interview Series, visit okawabooks.com

ABOUT HAPPY SCIENCE

Happy Science is a global movement that empowers individuals to find purpose and spiritual happiness and to share that happiness with their families, societies, and the world. With more than 12 million members around the world, Happy Science aims to increase awareness of spiritual truths and expand our capacity for love, compassion, and joy so that together we can create the kind of world we all wish to live in.

Activities at Happy Science are based on the Principle of Happiness (Love, Wisdom, Self-Reflection, and Progress). This principle embraces worldwide philosophies and beliefs, transcending boundaries of culture and religions.

Love teaches us to give ourselves freely without expecting anything in return; it encompasses giving, nurturing, and forgiving.

Wisdom leads us to the insights of spiritual truths, and opens us to the true meaning of life and the will of God (the universe, the highest power, Buddha).

Self-Reflection brings a mindful, nonjudgmental lens to our thoughts and actions to help us find our truest selves—the essence of our souls—and deepen our connection to the highest power. It helps us attain a clean and peaceful mind and leads us to the right life path.

Progress emphasizes the positive, dynamic aspects of our spiritual growth–actions we can take to manifest and spread happiness around the world. It's a path that not only expands our soul growth, but also furthers the collective potential of the world we live in.

PROGRAMS AND EVENTS

The doors of Happy Science are open to all. We offer a variety of programs and events, including self-exploration and self-growth programs, spiritual seminars, meditation and contemplation sessions, study groups, and book events.

Our programs are designed to:

* Deepen your understanding of your purpose and meaning in life
* Improve your relationships and increase your capacity to love unconditionally
* Attain peace of mind, decrease anxiety and stress, and feel positive
* Gain deeper insights and a broader perspective on the world
* Learn how to overcome life's challenges

... and much more.

For more information, visit happy-science.org.

ABOUT HAPPINESS REALIZATION PARTY

The Happiness Realization Party (HRP) was founded in May 2009 by Master Ryuho Okawa as part of the Happy Science Group. HRP strives to improve the Japanese society, based on three basic political principles of "freedom, democracy, and faith," and let Japan promote individual and public happiness from Asia to the world as a leader nation.

1) Diplomacy and Security: Protecting Freedom, Democracy, and Faith of Japan and the World from China's Totalitarianism

Japan's current defense system is insufficient against China's expanding hegemony and the threat of North Korea's nuclear missiles. Japan, as the leader of Asia, must strengthen its defense power and promote strategic diplomacy together with the nations which share the values of freedom, democracy, and faith. Further, HRP aims to realize world peace under the leadership of Japan, the nation with the spirit of religious tolerance.

2) Economy: Early economic recovery through utilizing the "wisdom of the private sector"

Economy has been damaged severely by the novel coronavirus originated in China. Many companies have been forced into bankruptcy or out of business. What is needed for economic recovery now is not subsidies and regulations by the government, but policies which can utilize the "wisdom of the private sector."

For more information, visit en.hr-party.jp

HAPPY SCIENCE ACADEMY JUNIOR AND SENIOR HIGH SCHOOL

Happy Science Academy Junior and Senior High School is a boarding school founded with the goal of educating the future leaders of the world who can have a big vision, persevere, and take on new challenges.

Currently, there are two campuses in Japan; the Nasu Main Campus in Tochigi Prefecture, founded in 2010, and the Kansai Campus in Shiga Prefecture, founded in 2013.

CONTACT INFORMATION

Happy Science is a worldwide organization with branches and temples around the globe. For a comprehensive list, visit the worldwide directory at *happy-science.org*. The following are some of the many Happy Science locations:

United States and Canada

New York
79 Franklin St., New York, NY 10013
Phone: 212-343-7972
Fax: 212-343-7973
Email: ny@happy-science.org
Website: happyscience-usa.org

New Jersey
66 Hudson St., #2R, Hoboken, NJ 07030
Phone: 201-313-0127
Email: nj@happy-science.org
Website: happyscience-usa.org

Chicago
2300 Barrington Rd., Suite #400,
Hoffman Estates, IL 60169
Phone: 630-937-3077
Email: chicago@happy-science.org
Website: happyscience-usa.org

Florida
5208 8th St., Zephyrhills, FL 33542
Phone: 813-715-0000
Fax: 813-715-0010
Email: florida@happy-science.org
Website: happyscience-usa.org

Atlanta
1874 Piedmont Ave., NE Suite 360-C
Atlanta, GA 30324
Phone: 404-892-7770
Email: atlanta@happy-science.org
Website: happyscience-usa.org

San Francisco
525 Clinton St.
Redwood City, CA 94062
Phone & Fax: 650-363-2777
Email: sf@happy-science.org
Website: happyscience-usa.org

Los Angeles
1590 E. Del Mar Blvd., Pasadena, CA 91106
Phone: 626-395-7775
Fax: 626-395-7776
Email: la@happy-science.org
Website: happyscience-usa.org

Orange County
10231 Slater Ave., #204 Fountain Valley, CA 92708
Phone: 714-659-1501
Email: oc@happy-science.org
Website: happyscience-usa.org

San Diego
7841 Balboa Ave., Suite #202
San Diego, CA 92111
Phone: 626-395-7775
Fax: 626-395-7776
E-mail: sandiego@happy-science.org
Website: happyscience-usa.org

Hawaii
Phone: 808-591-9772
Fax: 808-591-9776
Email: hi@happy-science.org
Website: happyscience-usa.org

Kauai
3343 Kanakolu Street, Suite 5
Lihue, HI 96766
Phone: 808-822-7007
Fax: 808-822-6007
Email: kauai-hi@happy-science.org
Website: happyscience-usa.org

Toronto
845 The Queensway
Etobicoke ON M8Z 1N6 Canada
Phone: 1-416-901-3747
Email: toronto@happy-science.org
Website: happy-science.ca

Vancouver
#201-2607 East 49th Avenue
Vancouver, BC, V5S 1J9, Canada
Phone: 1-604-437-7735
Fax: 1-604-437-7764
Email: vancouver@happy-science.org
Website: happy-science.ca

INTERNATIONAL

Tokyo
1-6-7 Togoshi, Shinagawa
Tokyo, 142-0041 Japan
Phone: 81-3-6384-5770
Fax: 81-3-6384-5776
Email: tokyo@happy-science.org
Website: happy-science.org

Seoul
74, Sadang-ro 27-gil,
Dongjak-gu, Seoul, Korea
Phone: 82-2-3478-8777
Fax: 82-2-3478-9777
Email: korea@happy-science.org
Website: happyscience-korea.org

London
3 Margaret St.
London, W1W 8RE United Kingdom
Phone: 44-20-7323-9255
Fax: 44-20-7323-9344
Email: eu@happy-science.org
Website: happyscience-uk.org

Taipei
No. 89, Lane 155, Dunhua N. Road
Songshan District, Taipei City 105, Taiwan
Phone: 886-2-2719-9377
Fax: 886-2-2719-5570
Email: taiwan@happy-science.org
Website: happyscience-tw.org

Sydney
516 Pacific Highway, Lane Cove North,
2066 NSW, Australia
Phone: 61-2-9411-2877
Fax: 61-2-9411-2822
Email: sydney@happy-science.org

Kuala Lumpur
No 22A, Block 2, Jalil Link Jalan Jalil
Jaya 2, Bukit Jalil 57000,
Kuala Lumpur, Malaysia
Phone: 60-3-8998-7877
Fax: 60-3-8998-7977
Email: malaysia@happy-science.org
Website: happyscience.org.my

Sao Paulo
Rua. Domingos de Morais 1154,
Vila Mariana, Sao Paulo SP
CEP 04010-100, Brazil
Phone: 55-11-5088-3800
Email: sp@happy-science.org
Website: happyscience.com.br

Kathmandu
Kathmandu Metropolitan City,
Ward No. 15, Ring Road, Kimdol,
Sitapaila Kathmandu, Nepal
Phone: 97-714-272931
Email: nepal@happy-science.org

Jundiai
Rua Congo, 447, Jd. Bonfiglioli
Jundiai-CEP, 13207-340, Brazil
Phone: 55-11-4587-5952
Email: jundiai@happy-science.org

Kampala
Plot 877 Rubaga Road, Kampala
P.O. Box 34130, Kampala, Uganda
Phone: 256-79-4682-121
Email: uganda@happy-science.org
Website: happyscience-uganda.org

ABOUT IRH PRESS

IRH Press Co., Ltd., based in Tokyo, was founded in 1987 as a publishing division of Happy Science. IRH Press publishes religious and spiritual books, journals, magazines and also operates broadcast and film production enterprises. For more information, visit *okawabooks.com.*

Follow us on:

Facebook: Okawa Books
Twitter: Okawa Books
Goodreads: Ryuho Okawa
Instagram: OkawaBooks
Pinterest: Okawa Books

NEWSLETTER

To receive book related news, promotions and events, please subscribe to our newsletter below.

eepurl.com/bsMeJj

OKAWA BOOK CLUB PODCAST

A conversation about Ryuho Okawa's titles, topics ranging from self-help, current affairs, spirituality and religions. Available at iTunes, Spotify and Amazon Music.

BOOKS BY RYUHO OKAWA

RYUHO OKAWA'S LAWS SERIES

The Laws Series is an annual volume of books that are mainly comprised of Ryuho Okawa's lectures that function as universal guidance to all people. They are of various topics that were given in accordance with the changes that each year brings. *The Laws of the Sun*, the first publication of the laws series, ranked in the annual best-selling list in Japan in 1994. Since, the laws series' titles have ranked in the annual best-selling list every year for more than two decades, setting socio-cultural trends in Japan and around the world.

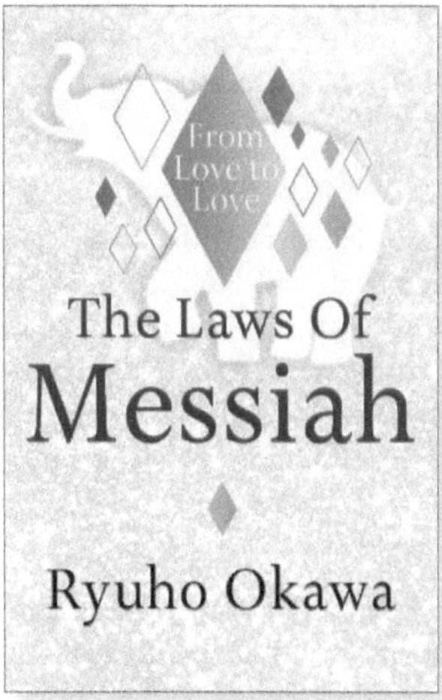

Scheduled to be published in January 2022

The 28th Laws Series

The Laws Of Messiah

From Love to Love

Paperback • 248 pages • $16.95
ISBN: 978-1-942125-90-7

"What is Messiah?" This book carries an important message of love and guidance to people living now from the Modern-Day Messiah or the Modern-Day Savior. It also reveals the secret of Shambhala, the spiritual center of Earth, as well as the truth that this spiritual center is currently in danger of perishing and what we can do to protect this sacred place.

Love your Lord God. Know that those who don't know love don't know God. Discover the true love of God and the ideal practice of faith. This book teaches the most important element we must not lose sight of as we go through our soul training on Earth.

For a complete list of books, visit okawabooks.com

THE TRILOGY

The first three volumes of the Laws Series, *The Laws of the Sun*, *The Golden Laws*, and *The Nine Dimensions* make a trilogy that completes the basic framework of the teachings of God's Truths. *The Laws of the Sun* discusses the structure of God's Laws, *The Golden Laws* expounds on the doctrine of time, and *The Nine Dimensions* reveals the nature of space.

THE LAWS OF THE SUN

ONE SOURCE, ONE PLANET, ONE PEOPLE

Paperback • 288 pages • $15.95
ISBN: 978-1-942125-43-3

IMAGINE IF YOU COULD ASK GOD why He created this world and what spiritual laws He used to shape us—and everything around us. If we could understand His designs and intentions, we could discover what our goals in life should be and whether our actions move us closer to those goals or farther away.

At a young age, a spiritual calling prompted Ryuho Okawa to outline what he innately understood to be universal truths for all humankind. In *The Laws of the Sun*, Okawa outlines these laws of the universe and provides a road map for living one's life with greater purpose and meaning.

In this powerful book, Ryuho Okawa reveals the transcendent nature of consciousness and the secrets of our multidimensional universe and our place in it. By understanding the different stages of love and following the Buddhist Eightfold Path, he believes we can speed up our eternal process of development. *The Laws of the Sun* shows the way to realize true happiness—a happiness that continues from this world through the other.

For a complete list of books, visit okawabooks.com

THE GOLDEN LAWS

HISTORY THROUGH THE EYES OF THE ETERNAL BUDDHA

Paperback • 201 pages • $14.95
ISBN: 978-1-941779-81-1

Throughout history, Great Guiding Spirits have been present on Earth in both the East and the West at crucial points in human history to further our spiritual development. *The Golden Laws* reveals how Divine Plan has been unfolding on Earth, and outlines 5,000 years of the secret history of humankind. Once we understand the true course of history, through past, present and into the future, we cannot help but become aware of the significance of our spiritual mission in the present age.

THE NINE DIMENSIONS

UNVEILING THE LAWS OF ETERNITY

Paperback • 168 pages • $15.95
ISBN: 978-0-982698-56-3

This book is a window into the mind of our loving God, who designed this world and the vast, wondrous world of our afterlife as a school with many levels through which our souls learn and grow. When the religions and cultures of the world discover the truth of their common spiritual origin, they will be inspired to accept their differences, come together under faith in God, and build an era of harmony and peaceful progress on Earth.

LAWS SERIES

THE LAWS OF SECRET

AWAKEN TO THIS NEW WORLD AND CHANGE YOUR LIFE

Paperback • 248 pages • $16.95
ISBN: 978-1-942125-81-5

Our physical world coexists with the multi-dimensional spirit world and we are constantly interacting with some kind of spiritual energy, whether positive or negative, without consciously realizing it. This book reveals how our lives are affected by invisible influences, including the spiritual reasons behind influenza, the novel coronavirus infection, and other illnesses. The new view of the world in this book will inspire you to change your life in a better direction, and to become someone who can give hope and courage to others in this age of confusion.

THE LAWS OF GREAT ENLIGHTENMENT

ALWAYS WALK WITH BUDDHA

Paperback • 232 pages • $17.95
ISBN: 978-1-942125-62-4

Constant self-blame for mistakes, setbacks, or failures and feelings of unforgivingness toward others are hard to overcome. Through the power of enlightenment we can learn to forgive ourselves and others, overcome life's problems, and courageously create a brighter future ourselves. This book addresses the core problems of life that people often struggle with and offers advice on how to overcome them based on spiritual truths.

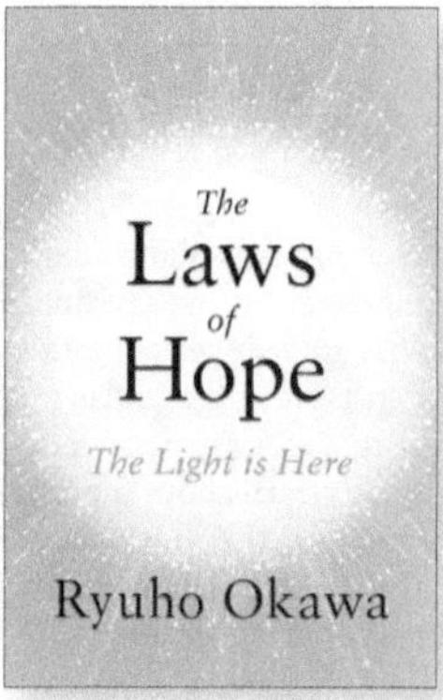

THE LAWS OF HOPE

THE LIGHT IS HERE

Paperback • 224 pages • $16.95
ISBN:978-1-942125-76-1

This book provides ways to bring light and hope to ourselves through our own efforts, even in the midst of sufferings and adversities. Inspired by a wish to bring happiness, success, and hope to humanity, Okawa shows us how to look at and think about our lives and circumstances. By making efforts in your current circumstances, you can fulfill your mission to shed light on yourself and those around you.

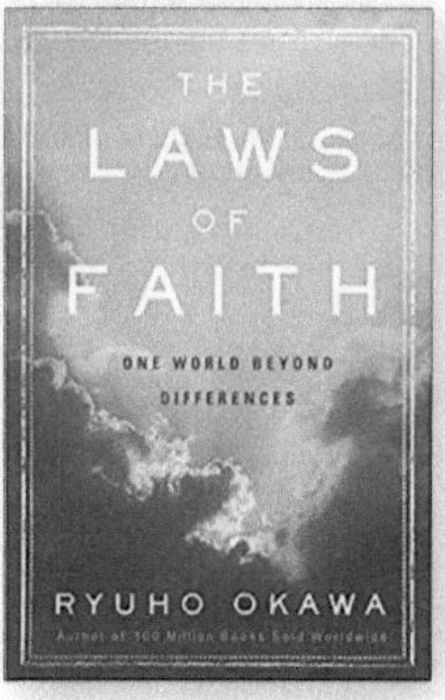

THE LAWS OF FAITH

ONE WORLD BEYOND DIFFERENCES

Paperback • 208 pages • $15.95
ISBN: 978-1-942125-34-1

Ryuho Okawa preaches at the core of a new universal religion from various angles while integrating logical and spiritual viewpoints in mind with current world situations. This book offers us the key to accept diversities beyond differences in ethnicity, religion, race, gender, descent, and so on, harmonize the individuals and nations and create a world filled with peace and prosperity.

MESSAGES FROM SPACE BEINGS

SPIRITUAL MESSAGES FROM METATRON LIGHT IN THE TIMES OF CRISIS

Paperback • 146 pages • $11.95
ISBN: 978-1-943928-19-4

Metatron is one of the highest-ranking angels (seraphim) in Judaism and Christianity, and also one of the saviors of universe who has guided the civilizations of many planets including Earth, under the guidance of Lord God. Such savior has sent a message upon seeing the crisis of Earth. You will also learn about the truth behind the coronavirus pandemic, the unimaginable extent of China's desire, the danger of appeasement policy toward China, and the secret of Metatron.

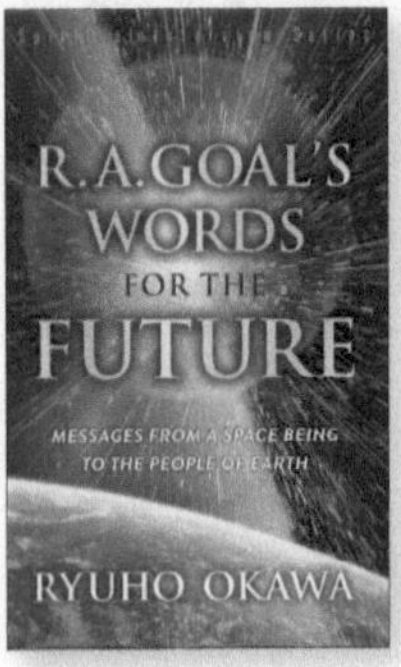

R. A. GOAL'S WORDS FOR THE FUTURE

MESSAGES FROM A SPACE BEING TO THE PEOPLE OF EARTH

Paperback • 174 pages • $11.95
ISBN: 978-1-943928-10-1

R. A. Goal, a certified messiah from Planet Andalucia Beta in Ursa Minor, gives humans on Earth three predictions for 2021. They include the prospect of the novel coronavirus pandemic, the outlook of economic crisis, and the risk of war. But the hope is that Savior is now born on Earth to overcome any bad predictions. Now is the time to open our hearts and listen to the words from R. A. Goal.

THE TRUE HEART OF YAIDRON

GUIDELINES FOR HUMANKIND SUFFERING FROM THE CORONAVIRUS

Paperback • 144 pages • $11.95
ISBN: 978-1-943928-04-0

What are the real cause and evil schemes behind the worldwide coronavirus crisis? Out of compassion, this book reveals truths about the all-out global war now being waged by the evil power in East Asia that's destroying the power of the people. Discover the movement that's trying to bring together the powers of the West, India, and Asia by the belief of "With Savior," to save humankind and create the new golden future of Earth.

CONSIDERING THE FUTURE OF THE WORLD

TRUMP SHALL NEVER DIE

HIS DETERMINATION TO COME BACK

Paperback • 206 pages • $11.95
ISBN: 978-1-943928-08-8

This book unveiled Mr. Donald Trump's true thoughts never reported by the media through spiritual interview with the guardian spirit of him. The topics include the "madness" found in GAFA and the mainstream media, Mr. Trump's views on the coronavirus vaccine and global warming, and the true aim of "Make America Great Again."

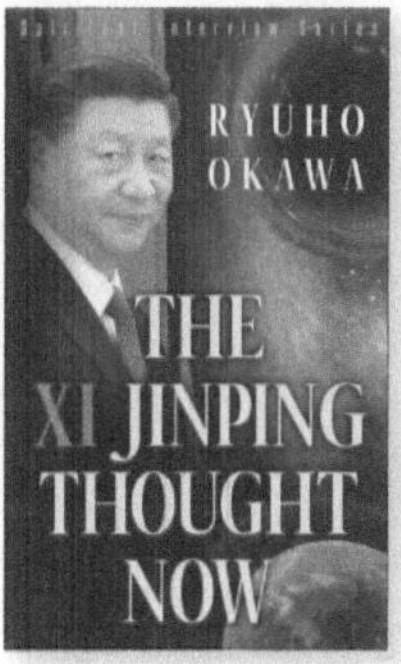

THE XI JINPING THOUGHT NOW

Paperback • 212 pages • $13.95
ISBN: 978-1-943928-05-7

With the launch of Biden administration in the U.S. and the 100th anniversary of the founding of the Chinese Communist Party approaching, China has been expanding its military threat and reinforcing its influence over the world. What urges China to seek global hegemony? This book unveils the "dark being" behind the Xi Jinping Thought.

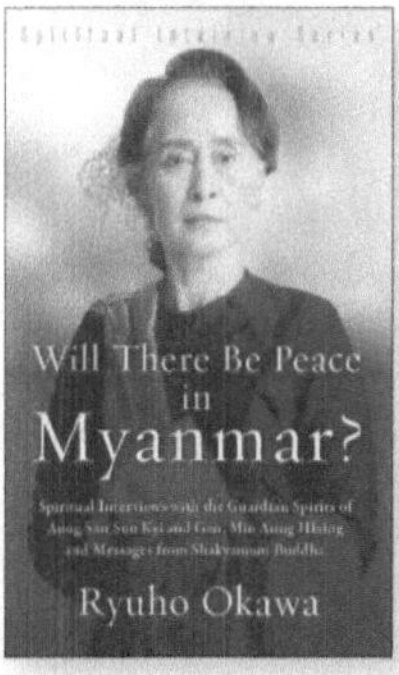

WILL THERE BE PEACE IN MYANMAR?

SPIRITUAL INTERVIEWS WITH THE GUARDIAN SPIRITS OF AUNG SAN SUU KYI AND GEN. MIN AUNG HLAING AND MESSAGES FROM SHAKYAMUNI BUDDHA

Paperback • 194 pages • $11.95
ISBN: 978-1-943928-12-5

February 2021. Tatmadaw, Myanmar Armed Forces, staged a coup against the pro-democracy leader Aung San Suu Kyi. Behind the nation's army lurks one of the world's major powers working to gain its influence on Myanmar. But, now is the time for the world to change. Words from Shakyamuni Buddha will also help bring peace to Myanmar, Asia, and the world.

For a complete list of books, visit okawabooks.com

HILIGHTED TITLE

THE ESSENCE OF BUDDHA

THE PATH TO ENLIGHTENMENT

Paperback • 208 pages • $14.95
ISBN: 978-1-942125-06-8

In this book, Ryuho Okawa imparts in simple and accessible language his wisdom about the essence of Shakyamuni Buddha's philosophy of life and enlightenment-teachings that have been inspiring people all over the world for over 2,500 years. By offering a new perspective on core Buddhist thoughts, Okawa brings these teachings to life for modern people. This book distills a way of life that anyone can practice to achieve a life of self-growth, compassionate living, and true happiness.

THE TEN PRINCIPLES FROM EL CANTARE VOLUME I

RYUHO OKAWA'S FIRST LECTURES ON HIS BASIC TEACHINGS

Paperback • 232 pages • $16.95
ISBN: 978-1-942125-85-3

This book contains the historic lectures given on the first five principles of the Ten Principles of Happy Science from the author, Ryuho Okawa, who is revered as World Teacher. These lectures produced an enthusiastic fellowship in Happy Science Japan and became the foundation of the current global utopian movement. You can learn the essence of Okawa's teachings and the secret behind the rapid growth of the Happy Science movement in simple language.

ROJIN, BUDDHA'S MYSTICAL POWER

ITS ULTIMATE ATTAINMENT IN TODAY'S WORLD

Paperback • 224 pages • $16.95
ISBN: 978-1-942125-82-2

In this book, Ryuho Okawa has redefined the traditional Buddhist term *Rojin* and explained that in modern society it means the following: the ability for individuals with great spiritual powers to live in the world as people with common sense while using their abilities to the optimal level. This book will unravel the mystery of the mind and lead you to the path to enlightenment.

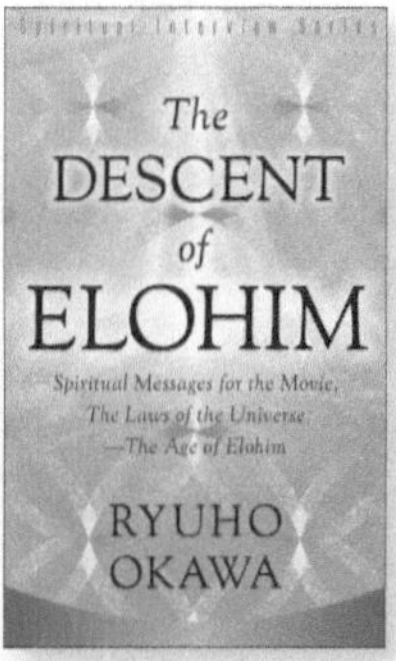

THE DESCENT OF ELOHIM

SPIRITUAL MESSAGES FOR THE MOVIE,
THE LAWS OF THE UNIVERSE-THE AGE OF ELOHIM

Paperback • 160 pages • $11.95
ISBN: 978-1-943928-17-0

This book contains the spiritual messages from Elohim, the Lord who appears in the Old Testament and who actually led His people about 150 million years ago. Through this book and the movie, *The Laws of the Universe - The Age of Elohim*, you can learn how life on Earth was like at that time, and how diverse people, who had come from other planets, fought each other until they finally found peace and harmony under Lord Elohim.

SPIRITUAL MESSAGES FROM THE GUARDIAN SPIRIT OF STAN LEE

ADVICE FOR *THE LAWS OF THE UNIVERSE - THE AGE OF ELOHIM*

Paperback • 200 pages • $11.95
ISBN: 978-1-943928-16-3

To seek advice on the plot for the movie *The Laws of the Universe - The Age of Elohim*, Okawa summoned the guardian spirit of Stan Lee, the father of Marvel Comics heroes. The guardian spirit of Stan Lee tells how he comes up with the heroes, and gives his insights on the kind of heroes that humans need in the coming Space Age.

HOW TO SURVIVE THE CORONAVIRUS RECESSION

Paperback • 171 pages • $14.95
ISBN: 978-1-943869-97-8

From the perspectives of both economics and health, this book delves into how you can survive the coronavirus recession. As taught by the author Ryuho Okawa, there is a strong relationship between your spiritual health and immunity, and he demonstrates the mindset you should have as well as introduces a very effective meditation that you can do to truly strengthen your immunity.

HOW TO BECOME A CREATIVE PERSON

WHAT WILL BECOME OF CORONAVIRUS PANDEMIC?
Readings by Edgar Cayce

UFOS CAUGHT ON CAMERA!
A Spiritual Investigation on Videos and Photos of the Luminous Objects Visiting Earth

THE LAWS OF SUCCESS
A Spiritual Guide to Turning Your Hopes into Reality

THE POWER OF BASICS
Introduction to Modern Zen Life of Calm, Spirituality and Success

WORRY-FREE LIVING
Let Go of Stress and Live in Peace and Happiness

THE STRONG MIND
The Art of Building the Inner Strength to Overcome Life's Difficulties

INVINCIBLE THINKING
An Essential Guide for a Lifetime of Growth, Success, and Triumph

THINK BIG!
Be Positive and Be Brave to Achieve Your Dreams

For a complete list of books, visit okawabooks.com

MUSIC BY RYUHO OKAWA

El Cantare Ryuho Okawa Original Songs

A song celebrating Lord God

A song celebrating Lord God,
the God of the Earth,
who is beyond a prophet.

➲ **Will be released in January 2022**

DVD
CD

The Water Revolution

English and Chinese version

For the truth and happiness of the 1.4 billion people in China who have no freedom. Love, justice, and sacred rage of God are on this melody that will give you courage to fight to bring peace.

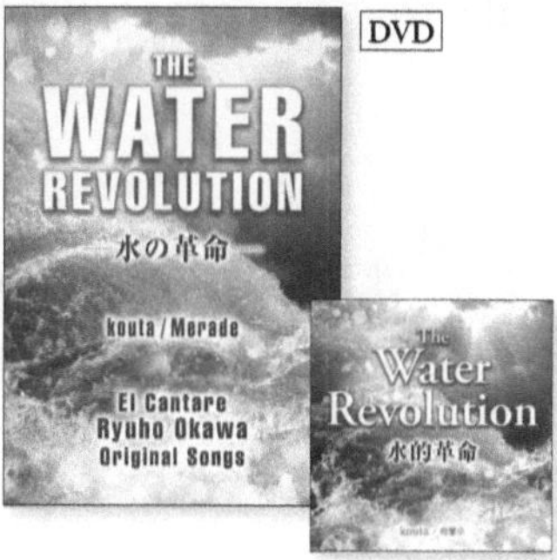

DVD
CD

Search on YouTube

the water revolution for a short ad!

Listen now today!

Download from
Spotify **iTunes** **Amazon**

DVD, CD available at amazon.com, and Happy Science locations worldwide

www.ingramcontent.com/pod-product-compliance
Lightning Source LLC
LaVergne TN
LVHW040145080526
838202LV00042B/3028
* 9 7 8 1 9 4 3 9 2 8 2 3 1 *